VISONS OF LIGHT
A COSMIC JOURNEY

Channelled by Joan Isaacs

PUBLISHED BY COSMIC DISC PUBLICATIONS

Published by Cosmic Disc Publications.
Printed by The Vale Press Ltd, Mickleton, Glos.

Cover illustration by Joan Isaacs.

ISBN 0-9523423-1-6

This book is dedicated

to the Cosmos

and to the Children of Light.

May their perfume spread widely.

Given in the year of 1994

The Mystic Flower
Has leaves of gold
And buds all time
Though ne'er unfolds
Its petals white
Except to whose
Who love its sight

The fragrance
Of the scented heart
Enfolds all those
Within it's path.
So lost are they
And may not move
So nectar filled
As not to choose.

The stem is of
a myriad souls,
Whose burning flame
Delights the whole.
Rooted deep within
the ground
It grows in grace
without a sound.

The fruit of this
Most heavenly flower
Is tasted only
In the hour
And blissful sweets
of paradise.

Introduction.

This book is the sequel to book one. It is comprised of three sections. The first section opens up the previous channelling found in book one. It furthers that channelling by detailed exposition and amplification pertaining to the soul, giving new information concerning its wholeness and fine connectedness to appropriate soul banding by showing its divine composition, comprehended within cycled incarnatory experiencing and ultimate Source return.

The second section shows ten prophecies which are placed within the central section of the book . This deliberation in sequence gives detailed information concerning certain possibilities which might eventually find final discharge if certain spiritual criteria remain unmet. The prophecies are not intended to spread "doom and gloom"; rather they carry a concealed salutary effect regarding spiritual incentive together with increased motivation to transmit more spiritual light and healing towards a severely damaged Earth which rests in critical phasing. If man's ability to discharge spiritual responsibility more effectively is strengthened by their reading, much advancement will have taken place towards the formation and creation of the new earth where man finally emerges as responsible guardian and spiritual being.

The third section dealing with tertiary channelling, gives the explanation for this particular type of channelling called visioning. The run down is set out in the preface pertaining to this section. Here the first person singular is used to denote the impersonal involvement of the channeller throughout. Symbolism is frequently used to signify the hidden and meaningful mode of the visions. These may be interpreted in different ways and form a useful guide for personal guidance within meditational practice.

We are entering into a new dimension which gives many faculties and gifts of a profound spiritual nature. The time in which we live is both exciting and thought provoking. We do have to go forward, for there can be no staying at the old third dimensional levels. We have grown up, shouldering new responsibilities for ourselves and our fellow man. Also the planet in which we presently live calls for transformation met within new dedication and commitment. Our lives will be amazingly changed! They will touch pertinently upon new ideals of service and love. Only within such fulfilment shall we declare ourselves to be truly children of the Cosmos and soul kin.

I enfold you all in great love and light.

Mickleton. 1994.

TABLE OF CONTENTS

Visioned channelling.

You began life as an emitted seed form which being breathed out by the Source, became a globe of pure and burning resonance. This was the original reflection of your soul. All heaven was mirrored in your clear vision, the magnificent breadth of which encompassed all galaxies. You returned always to praise the Creator into whose Eye you were held. Your brightness surpassing the Disc of Sun, outshone the brightest star. You were fashioned as a Cosmic being of light, having your abode within the orbit of timeless space. Your natural habitat being within the Cosmos itself found you always pleasing to the Creative and original thought in whose pure thought form you were fashioned.

In that day we spoke with you freely, and in that glory we beheld you as indeed you beheld us. Nothing was hidden, our close communication with you became myriad thought forms of spectrumed light which, spiralling and oscillating, rejoiced within the vortex of Universal sound and colour. Our frequencies blown full into the energies of the Cosmic wind breathed into your open soul sealing our angelic Union before the Source Itself.

There was joy then and in such abundance. Love was manifested fully in unparalleled beauty of flowering hours and fruiting seasons. We clothed you in the light raiment of kin and your investiture was that of Son and heir. This was pleasing and honourable to those of us who were of the Spirit and the seed of Universal thought.

It was your desire and choice to put off your glorious apparel for a time, donning the guise of the heavily encumbered earth man. This submission to lower dimensions was made in a spirit of loving service and sacrifice. You became the Cosmic Christs standing in every age for the reclamation of those souls who had sunk deeply into unspiritual ethos and darkness. Locked into dark energies and discovering no escape, finally fixed at this level, they would have been unable to return to a pristine and original state had it not been for your love and sacrifice which would ultimately redeem them.

1

You have travelled far since you left us many light years ago. We are still able to speak to you and our guidance and wisdom have remained open to you. Since you are now cloaked in earth energy, you have become immersed in that frequency and our transmissions do not always reach you. Part of your soul has temporarily closed to our light. If you were always aware of your true being, nature and connection, you could not complete these earth cycles without intense pain and an overwhelming nostalgia to return. So it has needed to be hidden from you until now.

The painful recognition and memory of your chosen separation from the Source is signalling strongly amongst many souls at this time. You are now able to accept this information with a spirit of joyfulness as you realize that your final journey is nearing completion and that we await your return in loving expectation. This is the breath of the Spirit who, giving understanding, inflames spiritual energy by spilling light into the awakening hearts of men. This new energy heralds the dawning of a new golden age when all will finally return to Source. Then the original status of man hall be fully restored. He will step once more into the pure light of the Source with greater soul enhancement and with multiple gifts in his outstretched hands. As he bows down before the throne of grace to make his offering he will be immediately uplifted to unsurpassed light and grace. Then all will be finally sealed to grace.

8th January 1994

Your soul names were bestowed upon you at the moment of the Great Creative Thought outpouring. These titles describe your unique, cosmically orientated birth, together with the measured and balanced equilibrium of matching soul nature. This energy emitted by the irradiated breath of Cosmic creativeness gave life and structure of form finally emerging as pure matter to clothe and nurture the spirit you eventually became.

After assuming spiritual guise, utterance was given in the shape of colour light and sound. This filled with enhanced Cosmic magnificence was further expressed in the form of homage realized in Cosmic outpouring. This became an acceptable offering from the created to the One Creative Original Thought or Mind. A phase of fused completion followed, witnessing to wholeness in the form of an undivided nuclei being experienced simultaneously within praise by the newly created soul and its Maker.

The soul filled with the stirrings of Divine Grace sought to express extended adoration of the Source in new and unparalleled generosity. Division of the original structure occurring by fission presently emerged by consensus as two equal and identical parts. Separation at two dimensional levels then ensued.

This division was made by deliberate choice. As part of the Self descended into the heavier vibratory energy of Earth, that other soul part remained permanently at Source level because there may not be one single moment in which Creator praise and adoration are interrupted. There always remains within the Heart of the Cosmos that vestige of energy which continues, whole, entire and unfragmented as an exact copy or replica of the original. It is also within this moment of chosen separation, a mere second in timelessness, that the action of return takes place. Then in joyful re-union the two soul parts become once more united, irreversibly re-fused as one undivided whole.

During the span of continued earth cycles, there is powerful realization and strong recognition as communication between each separate soul part takes place. Within these peak experiences love becomes overpowering as the spiritual generosity of the soul is experienced. This occurs momentarily in man during soul begraced moments where there is an abundant inflowing of spiritually charged energy. Such energy serves to bridge the two dimensional levels. Complete enlightenment during experiencing serves to gratify the Earth soul in its cycle of chosen and self-imposed separation from the original Source, reminding it of inevitable return.

In the joyous day of returning, the earth released soul aspires to rejoin its true counterpart, enriched and vibrationally raised, enjoying closer communion with the One Original thought. Then as both soul parts fuse, complementing one another, they are absorbed and eternally held within the ceaseless heart beat of magnified adoration. Then being fulfilled, the contract of witnessed experience at earth level is met and discharged. As each part unifies, it becomes absorbed into the all seeing single eye of emitted Creative energy enjoying total experience.

From its rightful place it signals to the collective soul force which now resurges to return by a powerful resonance that which meets within the spiritual core of all created matter. In returning to Source, all spiritually emitted energy resounds with great and sweet loving that individual harmonic note which ceaselessly sounds the name of the Creative Thought. May you enter into this peace.

11th January 1994

The pure vision of Cosmic consciousness is experienced by the soul as spiritual energy. Present in every particle of matter it is all knowing, all powerful and is directed towards the final realization of soul identity or expression. This energy which, is spirit, is housed temporarily within the physical body of man.

Man has the capacity for many bodies which are seen by The Cosmos as one ongoing spiritual journey with physical change to cell structure at metaphysical level. The body continues to deteriorate throughout mans earth cycles and this degeneration continues throughout the changing seasons of life. The infant grows into the child, the child develops into the man, the man matures, ages and finally dies, eventually discarding the present physical envelope. This evolutionary process is repeated in another vehicle until soul perfection is reached.

Man in spiritual journeying continues to express within his existence that energy which has neither beginning or end. This energy unlike the physical, cannot die since it is part of God Himself who is the Creative Source. God being pure consciousness, beholds man unfulfilled and incomplete until he has learnt to express that centre and spiritual nature which comprises all Universal energy in perfected order.

Until the soul reaches perfection, it may not be a part of that order. The higher self, which is spiritual energy unless expressed, is transferred to successive physical bodies for such purposeful action. The soul may inhabit many earth bodies although in spiritual substance remaining unchanged except for the action of grace which enlarges it.

Transparency of soul is accelerated when it moves from a separate state to merge with the universal movement of oneness; cosmically charged and mixing with all matter it is then fused into light creating one single energy. Then it reaches final absorption into the vortex of all ascending matter as part of returning and perfected energy which permanently enters the Source.

Man was created in order to enter into this perfected state of Universal order. In that ultimate state of elevation, he realizes the fullness of the Spirit. Then there is death to the Ego because he is emptied of all, embracing nothing except the Creative love which now draws him unresistingly towards the Source. All else becomes a mirage fading to reveal a state of pure spiritual consciousness. In that light alone he may view dispassionately the soul's total experience which seen through the single eye of the Cosmos has always militated towards joyful return. Form is then perfected standing as a permanent witness towards the single intent and original purpose of the Creative Thought.

12th January 1994.

There are many soul designate groups within the Cosmos, each discharging a specific energy and frequency. These form soul clusters, having identical Cosmic tasks to perform. All have conjointly reached maximum evolutionary levels after aeons of spiritual development. They are perfected light energies reflecting the aura of the Universal Source.

These souls continue with their main after-life task without interruption for millions of light years. Having become absorbed into Cosmic light, they are attracted to that Centre which is a reflection of themselves in the glorified and pure State of the Absolute Being.

Such pure souls may at given times elect and by common group consensus fulfil new tasks, this in response to changed or distorted patterns of energy which if uncorrected long term could undermine inter planetary balance within the Cosmic Whole.

The soul elect will SEND an emissary who will, by mutual agreement, complete an additional earth cycle with the express purpose of correcting such imbalance. This new contracting is outside the law of Karma since the old contract has already seen discharge within the soul's previous incarnatory experiencing.

The spiritual refashioning of disproportionate levels attaches then to that particular soul's accepted and extended life task to be discharged in circumstances where need has become urgently critical. Although the soul has chosen to undertake this task at Source level, it may have no knowledge of such at Earth level. There may or may not be partial knowledge of this especial responsibility occurring at some specific period within the life cycle.

The divulgence of such information makes entry into the time when action is both urgent and requisite; then there is proper divination of such messages together with a sense of great urgency to convey them appropriately. The recognition of the "Absolute truth" is given to the soul who comes to experience an awakening or sensing of accelerated Cosmic consciousness.

At no time is the elect made aware of its Cosmic soul banding, This will always remain hidden during earth cycles since the physical body with its lowered vibrational level would be unable to comprehend this information fully.

Once the contract is completed, the soul returns to the Source re-assuming its previous Cosmic task which is without interruption being eternally discharged by the myriad souls who have remained as part of the One Whole within the web of the Cosmos. All is one energy, one light.

12th February 1994

The contract of the soul within Super Consciousness becomes that of eternally resounding its own individual resonance and note. There are myriads of soul groupings, each within a particular strata or banding and at Cosmic level. All fall within the total harmonic and sequence of the Universal reverberation, carrying an identical soul vibration which is recognisable to other soul formations.

There is also a common structuring within Soul groups which is the cause of mutual attraction. This inducement results in Cosmic adhesion which connects all as one whole viable energy. Soul output within the Super Consciousnessness combines to amplify vibrational frequency. Collective energy is breathed into the mouth of the Source who enlivens it, then it is breathed out as spiritual energy. Spiritual gender is uniform within Cosmic indwelling.

This spiritual energy may descend at times to Earth levelling. When it does there is a quickened enlivening of super charged energy which, entering into the centre of man, raises and accelerates the soul to awakening at altered and higher dimensional level.

The higher the soul's vibratory capacity the more powerful the Cosmic note of Creative energy becomes. It is that energy of which he is always part. All then interacting sounds as one mighty crescendo entering into the mouth of the Harmonic Source and swelling Universal frequencies. In that single moment, there is oneness and singleness in all energised matter and perfected Adoration is both infinite and timeless.

This song of all Created beings is the psalmody of those souls whose vision and focus have centralised the Super Conscious within themselves, reflecting only the Source energy to which they are joined. They merge within this act of great spiritual intent together with all past, present and future identical soul groupings both above and below.

This pool of formative energy gathers to itself similar residual energy and is finally accessed into the form of pure light creating a diaphanous heaven upon earth which permits entry into all dimensions by virtue of increased soul growth and evolvement. The transparency of the purified and ascending soul reflects the light of the Cosmos itself. In its elevated state of inwardness it promulgates and seeds the active state of the Creative nucleus which confers immortality and timelessness.

When this circular process achieves fullness of completion, the cycle is endlessly repeated until all soul groupings at Cosmic level are permeated.

Given to Planet Earth 13th February 1994

All ongoing energy is finally realized within matter and form. Here its capacity is met and ultimately transformed. This energy then adapts to the salient features of its receiver host. Somewhere in the molecular structure there exists the module for the transceiver which follows a code of mimicked adherence. Similar to genetic DNA coding, energy becomes multiple to the single and original matrix.

An energy field is primarily distributive. It feeds itself out to similar modules, always regulating and adjusting, adhering to its original wave length. It is unable to vary followed patterning unless radical change to the overall blueprint or plan exists. So once an energy frequency is established, it is difficult to dislodge or alter its original vibratory level. Like attracts like!

This gives explanation to the belief that negativity begets itself and by so doing, amplifies its own energy. Until there is a contrary or opposing force field which is able to predominate, unseating the original or former energy, viable change is rendered impervious or obsolete.

Spiritual energy possesses a higher charge or frequency. Its field of irradiation is composed of Cosmically charged light particles which are effectively discharge or dissolve the electrical component and structuring of heavier lower energies. This catalytic action creates new electrical changes, re-forming the existing energy field whilst retaining its own inalienable and inviolable structure. The outcome of such change is spiritually positive!

Your planet Earth has long nourished and given birth to seed that, falling upon itself in bitter harvesting, serves to promote a dark energy which in turn lays waste, destroying and annihilating all within its pathway by amplifying its wholly negative nature and quality.

You are now faced with a new spiritual inquisitiveness which triggers a powerful predisposition towards the alternative indwelling and absorption of Cosmic light energy. This phases the dawning and realization of the spirit which is housed within the centre of man.

In consequence there now exists a state of war between positive and negative energy in which you as light bearers are engaged and presently committed. Negative energy is to be dis-armed and restructured to the Light if you are to Saviour your planet. This is the time when the Great Sword is unsheathed. Stand then as soul warriors and let the trumpet sound the victory into Infinite peacefulness. Go forth to birth the day when all men shall stand within Cosmic Light.

14th February 1994

Within the Universe there are many compositions of energy. Galactic spin is the foremost, controlling the oscillation and distancing of orbital substance. This Cosmic energy is the prime mechanistic movement in Space. Without its balance and distancing factor there would be substantial disturbance and collision between distributed and orbiting planetary systems.

The equation forwarded in maintaining this delicate Galactic balance over millions of years and even light years within those systems, and as yet inaccessible to man, is part of the Great Creative thought. This energy functions as constant motion, nevertheless it remains motionless at inner Source level since at the core of creation all remains silent within deliberative assembly and centering.

The Voice of the Creative Source mouths to a trillion energy frequencies of unuttered sound. Carried faster than the speed of light and within the resonance of its powerfully emitting path, it directs synchronous silence into the heart of all matter, birthing and fashioning the embryonic nuclei of existing formative energies. Sound travelling out with centrifugal force from the core or centre remains there at stilled level. Finding secondary expression which is sound within lesser energy it leaves the centre to move out to the peripheral outer surface which is ever evolving into matter. Returning again to remain at its original level it becomes re-absorbed into primary motionless action This silent energy force is constantly forming and re-forming out of prime Source energy.

Man is one of such fashioned and emitted energy forms. His soul is composed of a single spark of Divine Energy which will eventually emerge and seek return to the Source, being ignited and fired by pure soul desire. When this is realized, the soul will seek ultimate fusion and union to its created like.

The opening of soul consciousness recognises the loving impact of this Universal energy. Within wondrous contemplation man eventually recognises his own divinity seeing all contained within growing union of Creator and creature. Here the soul is met and held fast within the Silence of Create and Uncreate matter. In that moment fulfilment is experienced and there is knowledge of completed Oneness with all creative energy and resonance.

That light transmitted into your open hearts is the pure Light of Cosmic awareness and Absolute Truth. You are coming into the last cycle or phase in which all is to be given and received simultaneously. This heralds the advent of the fifth and subsequent dimensional levels.

15th February 1994

There is one intelligence governing and controlling every particle of issuing energy. This is the Universal Truth, the seat and centre of the Logos. Reflected in every way by the ordered Mind of the Creative Thought it is pure in intent and single in mindedness. Everything is reflected within this expression of creativity which is manifested through the Supreme Being as a reflection of Divine Energy.

Love is the key to Supreme awareness and knowing. You have only to release that energy or essence to change your world. The action of love energy is never effaced. Its joyful release issues from the eternal womb of the Source itself. Emerging from this pure energy of ordered intelligence, it issues forth as the Absolute Truth. Its return to Source displays the same pristine state and original energy. Such is the immaculate ordering of Universal laws governing all matter.

Man receives light directly from this Creative Thought of which he himself is a part. Upon him there is bestowed, as rightful son and heir, the deliberation of free choice. He may either fulfil a spiritual role as an earth dweller, acting within soul cycles as an integral container for Absolute Truth, or he may choose to deliberately move away. The greater distance between man and his Source, the more his disassociation with his true self. Without an input of love, there is no purposeful partnership with the Source. This becomes blocked. There there is a state of fragmentation where he is eventually faced with separation, no longer seeking perfection, and lacking incentive to be part of Universal intelligence and ordering. Within this state of evolutionary descent, he will become little more than the physical shell housing the primate.

The soul which rests within a spiritual state remains aligned to the Logos, its energy unaffected by lowered emotion or Ego projection. By maintaining contact with the Logos through the expression of the higher self, it is strongly linked to the Source throughout all subsequent earth cycles. There is always a growing inability to retain spiritual height within lower levels into which man often declines. These states lower soul vitality and spiritual wholeness. Then there is a loss of the higher self leading to fragmentation of all enjoining selves. Man prevented from ongoing process and completion of his evolutionary journeying, will need to touch in again upon former states when he was more deliberately aligned to spiritual wholeness.

The awakening of the Soul links to that original state wherein the spiritual is the head of the corporate body of man. Then all action is coloured by an energy which is Source orientated. There is strong motivation to align action to Divine Love, the key to multi dimensional entry. Initiated into the mainstream of Universal order, he may then assume conferred Angelic status. To awaken is to finally make return.

18th February 1994

When Source light permeates form and matter by entering into it spiritually, that becomes the day of Ascension for the soul elect. When there is total recognition of all experience as part of an evolutionary journey and loving initiation, then there is Ascension. When you perceive the Christ essence in others and reach out to all men in great spiritual love, then there is also Ascension.

The seed lying dormant in fertile soil is open to light. It is awakened by a tide of energy breathing into it the essence of life, promoting and quickening growth. As it moves towards that light source it is activated, dependant upon the force of nature to achieve maturity. First the stirring and swelling within the earth, then the tender shoots and leaves emerge. As the sap ascends upwards at its highest point buds form, these quickening to ultimate flowering and fruiting. That cycle then realizes completion. This is followed by a period of resting as similar cycles of growth follow.

Man follows this pattern of natural growth. He is created as consciousness in form, the highest point of soul maturation occurring within incarnatory cycles. This, dependant upon his stage of evolution or expanding consciousness, is coupled to a sense of increasing spiritual responsibility. With the raising of consciousness, there is freedom from former constraints which have retained him at lower level. He is then able to enter into new dimensions of Super Consciousness which permit personal Ascension.

As the soul continues within its new expression of mobile spirituality, there is recognition of that higher consciousness which faces all existing matter towards the heart of Creative Thought. This pure vibration is found pulsating within all energy forms. The action of grace transfigures and uplifts matter towards its living centre with great dignity and laudability. This is the final phase and culmination of the ascended soul.

Present third dimensional energies are experienced by many souls as contributing towards the diminution of enlarged spiritual expression. This is a prohibitive process which must be examined in the light of new planetary energies which are "sweeping clean" past conditioned patterning, creating great purification to former eroded and faulty DNA encodement. Within this process former spiritual metamorphosis is eliminated. This is the transient phase wherein the new spirituality of man is comprehended and fully realized.

It is within this evolutionary jump from third to fifth dimension that change in form is consequently raised and enlivened in order to adapt to this new shift in heightened super consciousness. The changeover point is critical, for all existing life forms must pass through this particular Cosmic Portal. Those souls who have awakened and opened to Cosmic light, will experience easing into the New dimensional path without excessive shock to the etheric or subtle bodies. Vibrational uplift presently experienced as heightened sensitivity will become absorbed without excess of fear or anxiety. This interchange will access into the newly formed light body with its Cosmically aligned and receptive frequencies. For those souls who have chosen to close to ongoing spiritual charge and are conditioned to third dimensional existence with its materialistic values, the changeover point may be traumatic and excessive. These souls will have little or no insight into oncoming change due to lack of development within the higher self. Many will become disorientated showing gross imbalance and disturbance as the new energies are experienced. Many will be assisted throughout this stressful event by souls discharging further service contract. This has been set out in previous channelling.

Form is now emerging into refined and purer form. This being represented by a circular Universal movement without beginning or end (Alpha and Omega) and into which souls enter, spiral, and are subsequently transfigured. Soul maturation finds entry into Super Conscious states which are the open portals for future dimensional and spiritual kingdoms. Awakened man now touches pertinently upon his own resurrection and final Ascension. Endless praise and Adoration to the Source who is the Centre indwelling within each soul.

20th February 1994

15

W hat you have retained during third dimensional experience will prove invalid as you enter fifth dimensional phasing. Realized experience at latter levels will indicate simultaneous combination of both left and right brain hemispheres. This balanced function will lead to appreciable and quickened acceptance of new dimensional learning processes.

All related experience will be intercepted by the higher self or awakened subconscious mind. This silent area of the brain largely dormant by third dimensional man and now awakened stands as monitor and guardian to the new brain bifurcation. This contains the division of two main branches whose function it is to act as receptor and interpreter to incoming and outgoing Cosmic signals and frequencies.

The altered bifurcation of brain relays and feeds into the main stem changed frequencies to sound and colour; the new range will be greatly enhanced and highly sensitized These altered levels cannot be interpreted at present third dimensional level. Hearing in the fifth dimension will extend and amplify, receiving sound over greater distances, together with an ability to interpret the signalled sound of all existing energy forms. This will move towards greater communication and deeper understanding between man and interplanetary systems. The new dimensional acoustics will develop from the present auditory system.

Colour will be seen contained within the Cosmic spectrum and new colour bandings together with their unique vibration will be signalled into an altered optical system. Assisting the fine fibres of the eye to adapt to extended vision there will be an ability to see from all angles. This will present without shock or disruption to the nervous system. Changes of this nature will gradually take place within fully monitored and protective programming. Ultimately the present mode of single vision will open to full Cosmic vision, this will facilitate towards comfortable interchange at multi-planetary level.

Such development has always been envisaged by us as an essential part of the evolutionary process. Man is made ready to move into this new phase where there is an expansion of the higher consciousness. Then he may move freely upwards towards total realization of the spiritual self. When consciousness opens fully, there will be a resulting lightness and motivation towards spiritual values, this resulting from a purification process which clears malfunctioning DNA. We have to tell you that much of your acquired and learnt knowledge will be useless on entry to this new dimension. You will be as little children involved in a new learning process, previously unknown. There is much to discard by way of the encumbrance of third dimensional experience which if not released could impede or block progress and subsequent entry into the higher dimensional states.

Many out of fear will choose not to go forward. They cannot remain however at their present stage of development. All are required to enter into the new fifth dimensional state and within an allocated time span. All souls are enabled to attempt this quantum leap if they are carried upon the great tide of heart essence which awakened and loving souls are now releasing. Such is the powerful charge of this energy that all within its light path may dare to ascend. Then in absolute trust and in the total absence of fear, all men will enter through this Cosmic portal.

We stand in your time to serve. 22th February 1994

The indwelling soul is the receptacle for Divine Grace. Grace is the finalized action of soul-light. The seat of the soul is held at Source or Logos level; it is not retained within the physical for any indeterminable period. Released from its temporary container, it returns to its first origins whose abode is outside temporal time. Fashioned from spiritual energy, it is fired by Source energy.

17

When it is ultimately released from earth experience within lower frequencies, it returns to the Cosmos. Here it recounts all experience within completed planetary cycles which are held against the backdrop of enquiring immortality. Then there is the chosen moment of return, this being sought in order to satisfy fullest expression to the Creative First Thought in whose image and likeness it is formed. When this expression is fully gratified, then the process of evolutionary journeying is complete. Only then is the soul permanently homed and re-admitted to Source Light.

Balanced soul energy is always matched to the degree of emerging and returning energy. There is never a fraction of imbalance. Such are the requirements of Universal laws governing cause and effect. The original state of the soul is unaffected by experience at lower planetary level, it returns to the Source in pristine state. Some souls required to journey long, touching into many solar systems for varied experience before returning. Others experience less by way of Earth sojourn and are quickly re-admitted to Source. Each soul has an individual contract within the ordering and perfection of Universal distribution. The original contract is effective until discharged. It remains within all incarnatory cycles until Karmic contracting is effected.

Super conscious states occur within final stages of evolutionary development. Fusion and union of soul and temporal body unite to spill out, even at conscious levels, peak moments of ecstasy and Divine love. These communicate to the fullest expression of radiating soul-light. This manifests as a transparent flame emerging from the creatured form. It is then the soul shines out of the created counterpart, transfusing and spiritually aligning both within a new partnership. Then the physical rests within perfect balance. The soul by spiritual cueing addresses itself to that overall balance.

Since the soul is composed of intangible qualities, it is not subject to the law of the physical and chemical body in which it temporarily resides. Whereas the earth body carries the penalty of death, there is strict conformity to that governing principle. The soul is the portal of immortality.

These two components, one spiritual the other earth formed and temporal, come to reside and experience under the same roof at different dimensional level. Man is awakening to his soul in this millennium. As he touches into this powerful centre he will become spiritually transfigured, and, the earth body will take on the resplendent quality of soul-light which is the token sign of an ascended spirit. Man is then elevated at both human and spiritual level.

23rd February 1994

Within the mind is planted the seed of pure Cosmic thought. This will grow, germinating within a climate of spiritual awareness, yielding a harvest so great that all partake of its generosity and plentiful abundance. The light of the Cosmic Sun shining into the hearts of souls illuminate and warm the new seed as it lies sleeping in the dark, making it over into light. New energies emerge which are the fruit of this seed. They carry sustenance to the awakened soul endowing it with great spiritual empowerment. All thoughts and words these souls transmit will be spiritual in essence. By the powering of Cosmically enhanced sound, they by addressing themselves to others will transmit future seed to those who shall witness the dawning of the fifth dimension which is spiritual light.

You are raised up, you are glorified. The spirit of air, fire, water and earth enter your soul. You are come together in these elements, part of all things, yet remaining as one. Gifts of prophecy shall be given in the latter days. The mind, visioning the wondrous light of the Cosmos, will delight in reflecting the soul light of countless generations who open to its burning flame. You are become the truth itself, and anything not of this pure energy shall fail. It will not seed itself to harvest.

You are covered with the shield of the spirit, you shall cry with a loud voice to the soul within you. It will answer you in deeds of compassionate overseeing. Now clothed in soul vesture you may stand within that day of ascension. The holy place becomes your habitat. You dwell with angelic beings. No thought is hidden from you, you look into the hearts of many witnessing to great loving and understanding. All who come to you do so as equals. All are leaders, all are prophets, all are come into spiritual light!

You stand up as the rightful servant and messenger of peace. All who look upon you will admit your thoughts, seeding them into their minds. You will cast waves of Cosmic light into their hearts, this germinating its like to a multiplicity of awaiting souls. We have clothed you in our thoughts, you are made resplendent with their light. Our resonance stirs within your heart. We have named you to stand before all people.

Our words cannot fade from your mind. They are impregnated deeply within your soul. They are made fast into timelessness. You will recognise them by the essence and the energy of love they carry. These words may be given to souls who receive new life from their empowering charge. They come to all men from the pure breath of the Source Itself who gives them form, emitting them in loving creativeness. We are charged to carry this breath into your darkened world as globes of Cosmic light. This light will inflame all souls with Cosmic fire. This fire will consume all which is unspiritual, leaving only the pure gold of spiritual enlightenment.

In earlier channellings, we addressed you as "the elect", "the chosen", the "God vessels" Some souls closed to these words since they were absorbed at Ego level only. Had they been admitted at higher self level and to the soul, there would have been commensurate understanding, and acceptance in humility of spirit. We address these titles to you once again and to the spiritual self. This is the soul which has in joyfulness participated throughout all evolutionary cycles towards its own Divine Choosing. We greet you as soul kin.

24th February 1994

The zenith of the soul at its culminating point lies within the capacity to emit an individual Cosmic note. When this is formulated, there is immense joy in heaven. All Universal energies bending towards this sound, declare an uniqueness which surpasses all other frequencies. Its resounding resonance penetrates all vibrational levels as it declares its emerging and glorified state of triumphant re-entry to the Source.

Within this transparent light all darkness finally flees. The veil of flesh parts to reveal eternal beauty of an immortal quality. This, sanctified, is made holy through pure enhancement of spiritual thought and perfected desiring.

Let the joyful Anthem sound, the victor returns victorious without the spoils of war. The outcome of peace is stronger than the dulling weapons of warring armies. Let the silence ring with wordlessness that endless song which is begotten of love itself. This is the completion of the last cycle.

We surround the returning soul with great watchfulness and with tender vigilance. That which is given in absolute trust shall be carried in love to the breath of the Cosmos by cohorts of angelic beings whose essence perfumes the Universe to purifying soul fragrance. We are those guardians, the silent watchers who stand in sight of the journeying of every single soul. We bow low before its peaceful unctions and quiet benedictions realizing the profoundity and wideness of its immeasurable spirit.

Then there is the incense of profound and breathless adoration as the soul uplifted is blessed and enfolded within the great Universal pulse of all Creative thought. There is mirrored in that one moment the passing of all ages which gloriously hymn the praise of the Creator. Praise to His name.

25th February 1994

All souls within earth cycles are united, fretted and joined by invisible seaming to the main energy grid. This joining forming a common soul energy field is distributed at central Source level along fine lines which spread out as an invisible web across Universal space. Soul fusion binds all together in one protective and common uniformity of spirit.

Spiritual cohesiveness acting as a network, resembles the central nervous system of the physical body. Fine energy lines contribute collectively to feed and connect with the soul at all its spiritual levels during cycles of separation from the Source by maintaining it throughout at lowered earth frequencies. This line of spiritual ingestion feeding and nurturing the soul is unobservable at present third dimensional levels. It will, however be, manifested to many entering fifth dimensional states within future phasing.

Then it will be seen emerging as a luminous web of fine light fibres saturated and imbued with spiritual substance. This substance feeds and nurtures each soul during separation from the Source, binding all together as one common soul identity. The spiritual nature of this heavenly Manna was given to the Israelites during their sojourn in the desert which lasted for many years. They were entirely fed upon a spiritual food whose sustenance gave them life at two levels, one physical and the other spiritual, both complementary to one another.

When the soul completes a cycle of evolutionary experiencing, it detaches itself from this Universal web and is freed to re-ascend to Source. This delicate disconnection is made without excessive movement or disturbance to remaining soul groupings. The gap is then closed and sealed, although not until the replacing soul has descended to earth substituting for the soul who has ascended. The etheric umbilical cord remains attached to soul nature until it becomes finally emmeshed into the pulse of eternal energy. Here it attains a state of independency forming to pure Cosmic light and existing outside the overall protectiveness of any former nutritive attachment necessary during its total life within earth cycles.

This constant motion and process of ascending and descending souls moves freely within this vast protective network in which all are etherically joined as one until they become ready to move into the higher energy of the Cosmos itself. Then they become as soul worlds existing independently within their own light. These are the bright new stars shining within the oscillating motions of Universal space and timelessness.

26th.February 1994

The soul is constantly drawn towards new dimensions of Cosmic awareness. It has a new understanding of its ultimate destiny which is to rest within the heart of the Source. Since the inception of this concept, there has been a growing recognition of the new clarity which is entirely disposed towards spiritual inclination. As man awakens he is caught up within this new spirit of spiritual expansiveness. It is within these states of expanding consciousness that he is in realistic touch with the soul. This overlord speaks to him at powerful levels and he must acknowledge its overall guidance in deepening spiritual enquiry.

When man realizes the necessity for the platform of Universal laws and accepts the nature of these laws, he begins fully to comprehend that Divine Plan which purports to the ultimate perfection of all created and evolving matter of which he is a minute although integral part. He then chooses by an act of volition to incline his will towards this process of evolution, becoming strongly motivated to discharge these goals within each incarnatory cycle. His sole motivation to please the Creative Thought is surrounded by an increase in grace, promoting greater spiritual desirement.

There is a stillness within the centre of man, and this is communicated to those with whom he comes into contact. This inner silence or peace is the powerful energy of a soul resting completely within the action of Divine Love. There can be no higher aspirational state. Man is elevated, participating towards higher dimensional indwelling which finally and fully expresses his divinity. This is soul purposing or enlightenment.

Awakening of souls during the last phase will accelerate allowing for the maximum number of those who have completed incarnatory experience at third dimensional levels. These will facilitate fifth dimensional entry. This dimension may be experienced at Earth levelling providing there has been sufficient schooling within other spiritual states. Such may have been fulfilled by contracting within other planetary systems. We are in the process of setting before you the nature and function of the soul. Knowledge may now be admitted at conscious levels. The storing of soul information will consequently be absorbed into the left and right hand hemispheres of the brain. This will quicken spiritual enquiry.

Over the last year we have seen commitment to programmes which facilitate the New Cosmic frequencies. These energies now firmly established are circulating on Planet Earth. Some may prove disruptive to many souls and so our task of distributing these in stable inwave, assists many into their easy absorption without undue stress or discomfort. In time they will be accommodated comfortably within the subtle bodies becoming increasingly acceptable to the physical. All must pass through this portal of change, even those who wish to remain within the present third dimension. These souls will experience difficulty in adapting to change since they will have acquired little by way of insight or understanding into patterns of accelerated and unstable planetary conditions. Their capacity to exist within the new climate will be severely limited. For those who have contributed little towards their own spiritual growth will come to reap a bitter harvest.

27th February 1994

24

When the sound of the Cosmic Note is emitted it will be heard as a pure and single vibratory chord. Consisting of all uttered and unuttered frequencies it will resound, resonating into all awakened hearts. Then, meeting expression within higher sound frequencies and acting as multiple waves of light energy, it will gather all souls to be held fast as one soul within loud and triumphal outpouring. Within this entry the soul will attune to one single Universally emitted note. This note ultimately expanding to include all others, comes to widest expression in full harmonic orchestration wherein every living soul is re-admitted to the Source in overwhelming speed and carried in petitioned utterance.

This sound is light energy travelling upon countless waves of high Cosmic frequencies. It will explode into a single note of unprecedented urgency, expressing its total chromatic scale powerfully so that all matter responding to its joyous oscillation, and opening, will receive its frequency. A polyphonic sound net pulsing from the lowest vibrational key to the highest frequency in undulating waves of Cosmic light will create elevated transformational expression by the pure intonation of vibrational sound. This note will continue, resounding to the four corners of the Universe until the last soul is returned and eternally held within its spiralling vortex.

The frequency of the note emulates the first Creative sound which resounded across space and time, its ongoing memory serving to perpetuate the original thought of First Creative Parenting, magnetizing and drawing all souls towards its remembered orchestration. It was upon this sound wave that the original form of the soul was carried and subsequently emitted. Its signalling is powerfully recalled throughout all subsequent cycles. Now it calls upon the soul to return to that first and original Creative Thought from whence it was called forth and emerged.

Man has subconsciously remembered the Cosmic note throughout all subsequent incarnations, although its urgency is now heard with increased and greater insistency. The time for all souls to return to Source is soon to witness completion. Man is now becoming sensitively aware of this note and within the deepest reaches of the subconscious mind, he hears it clearly and as at no other time during total evolutionary journeying. It is the given signal to return to the Universal Creative womb who called him forth from nothingness into Created matter and form. His spiritual response towards this Cosmic sounding within the soul inevitably moves him forward and upwards into the realms of the Super conscious of which he is explicit expression.

Spiritual gifts are given to those who actively seek and desire them. In unselfish generosity the soul comes to desire the light of imparted grace within others of similar motivation and disposition. Then realized union is powerfully enlarged when grace becomes amplified within common soul grouping and identity. This manifests to the consolidation of collective spiritual energy which, transforming galaxies, realizes the spiritual elevation of all create matter within dimensions whose composition is composed of pure light energy. Light is the sole expression and manifestation of the Logos. Light and sound combine to magnify His Being.

1st March 1994

P resent energy levels have been elevated in order to absorb the new Cosmic frequencies. For many of you this will be a period of preparation leading towards a higher threshold in mental activity. All will gradually adapt to the intake of vibrationary input and output. For a time there could be noticeable fluctuation or swing together with experience of increasing instability and disorientation as these higher frequencies effect balance within the physical. In some there will be greater disruption than in others, dependent upon the cross over point in individual energy fields. A critical centering in situations where the energies of others are experienced as discordant or unmatched should be noted as this is of vital importance. All souls are in process of absorbing this new energy flow. Excess energies may be off loaded involuntarily finding ready housing within systems already overloaded. Frequent exercise in grounding techniques are necessary to maintain a comfortable point of balance. All incompatible energy should be redirected towards the Universal frequency which will eventually neutralize these towards more favourable output.

Healers especially should be more than usually vigilant. They should be aware that negative energy excess is moving at fast and accelerated speed, expelled as waste from many souls, only to find alternative accommodation in other human vehicles! Therefore the use of the hands should be avoided in healing programmes as these serve to conduct unwanted energy into many receptive and open channels through primary touch. We ask you to consider future healing as being directed solely by and through the mind. This is an altogether safer vantage-point and will be used in all future Cosmically orientated healing practice. Consider the advantages and adapt to this technique; it will afford you maximum protection from the increasing risk of unfavourable overloading.

Above all these times call for greater discernment. Incompatible energy spilling over from those who are insufficiently grounded or lacking in spiritual evolvement may carry over to others, giving rise to wounding within the etheric or subtle bodies.

Those mainly affected will be the sensitive or psychic, where thresholds of sensitivity are heightened. Such is the open state of the spiritually conscious at present that greater discernment and awareness is requisite for ongoing protection. In time powerful protection will be immediately afforded through the medium of the emerging and strengthening light body. This when fully developed will deflect unsought energies towards channels and polarities which will effectively neutralize them. Until that light body is made resolute, great care should be taken in the light of many destructive and prevailing energy patterns now in evidence.

The spiritual pivotal is at present in delicate and critical balance. There is of necessity a new openness which is presently allowing for the ongoing infusion of new energies. Until this process has seen completion, the etheric and subtle bodies are open ended to receive the higher frequencies. This in turn will affect the physical, mental and emotional bodies which are receiving this charge and at accelerated level. This is a temporary phase and will eventually balance out to completely acceptable and safe level. There will occur the right timing when the systemic structure may be safely re-sealed having absorbed the requisite content and necessary input of incoming new energies. This is expedient within the phase of intentional mutational change.

It is important for souls to understand this process of transitional change, since all will be affected in varying ways. The information we are giving has always been understood by the subconscious mind. Now it will be found to be acceptable at conscious levels due to the increase of spiritual awareness and expansiveness of soul awakening. Trust and loving acceptance are the key which opens the portal of Cosmic consciousness to all aspiring souls.

2nd March 1994

Many portent signs will be revealed before the advent of future events which could culminate in an unfavourable outcome. If man is prepared to communicate with his higher self within the interim period, contacting that self purposefully by directing his energy towards spiritual goals, this will call into existence an increased propensity towards positive energy together with new hope for an eventual and favourable outcome.

We wish you to consider how man by ongoing and destructive programming towards the natural law will eventually unleash a tide of bitter destruction. He will encounter the force and fury of nature which ultimately rebounding, shall fall most unfavourably upon him and future generations. This will be evidenced by the motivation of men who have only unspiritual desires at heart. The negative energy they expel can no longer secure for the Planet that stability whereby the natural yield of earth is assured. There will be continued imbalance as man attempts to implement that which he knows to be false action, and which is opposed towards the well being of earth dwellers. Deceit and subterfuge come to be clearly shown in their real light of lowered intention. Man forwarding such programmes is made responsible especially if such action serves to gratify and forward materialistic ends.

Your world as we see it is largely coloured by greed. Your rulers are men who are their own beginning and end. They have already ravaged many areas of earth. Due to their greed, many starve in the light of uncertain harvesting due to a massive disposal of natural resources sold in barter to wealthier nations. This brings waves of disease and death to those countries now existing in primary poverty and in famine conditions. Such action is due to the uncaring attitude of men who profit from the wealth of impoverished countries, selling natural resources for their own monetary advantage. Many perish in the tide of discrimination, which selects as ethnically unclean groupings with differing belief systems. This is strongly significant in ethnic minorities. All these things stand as warning signs of greater disruption to come.

Man has become the greatest predator of his own kind. Is it this unspiritual man who now attempts to protect your earth against invasion from natural bodies in outer space? If this is so, then there will be the same selective marketing process which will favour some and condemn others. This will be be seen within all future space programming.

The natural balance and gravity field of your planet has seen uninterruption from outer space for many years. Apart from small isolated incidents where matter from space has fallen to Earth infrequently the period of greatest danger to your planet took place in an earlier phase of formation, when there was massive upheaval within distribution of matter. This cycle is now quiescent.

With the rapid increase of life upon earth, this will witness the birth of an unnatural cycle where Man pits his intelligence more directly against the forces of nature. This action will serve to distribute even more unfavourably, giving priority to programmes where artificial intelligence is heavily in use. It is this intelligence which will eventually militate against him causing the holocaust and aftermath he presently fears.

All present disaster primarily caused by the action of "getting, having man" stands in direct opposition to the natural law. The grim results convey a climate of great chaos. They indicate man moving towards cataclysmic earth changes which if not halted could destroy present life upon Earth. Man is presently carried upon this destructive wave and towards his own decimation.

We speak finally of the asteroid belt which may be partially observed by man. The main belt cannot be seen as it is outside Earth's range. Man now actively seeks to effect asteroid deflection, and away from the vicinity of his planet. Artificial intelligence is to be harnessed in this neutralization programme which will shift these natural substances. Asteroids until now have caused little danger to earth. The residue of natural disintegration falls mainly into outer space and that part which does not is small, posing a minimum threat to the Planet.

Due to space programming and man's future plans promoting the prospecting of space territory, thought is being given to the removal of obstacles which could obstruct or delay such programming. The asteroid is not a risk to earthmen, but rather viewed as an obstacle in space where a race for clear spaceways of the future and the safety of space borne craft and passengers is presently unresolved.

This need on the part of man to clear everything out of the way in the name of progress is heavy with disaster. In clearing pathways in outer space, the asteroid is seen as removable debris. Any man made attempt to deflect it in its natural course and orbiting, will however assemble towards a massive collision affecting earth at terrible and unimaginable levels. Such action would finally result in the splitting of matter and energy which will then decimate your planet. Man will draw upon himself the full effect of the natural law which he consistently abuses and which has until now accommodated him at more or less reasonable levels. These laws in man made reversion will conduct to inevitable planetary extinction.

Only when man acts in love can he protect and nurture his own environment.

4th March 1994

We have formed a circle of light which now completely encompasses your planet. The structure of the circle is composed of striated bands of colour emanating from the heart of the Cosmic Spectrum. Each colour contains a frequency which is positively linked to a particular Source energy. This energy is Cosmically protective, deflecting from further invasional damage caused by incompatible vibrational wave.

The concentric nature of Cosmic energy waves are cushioning the planet against excessive shock from malformed frequencies circulating earth.

These are caused by aggravation locked into undischarged, residual negativity. This density is accumulating at both polarities which have now become saturated with negative and inert energy. This is producing a slowing down effect at the lower end of the polarity which has eventually resulted in instability at its axial point. This unfavourable situation must be corrected and re-stabilized.

The properties inherent in Cosmic energy carry the essence of pure Light rays. These are suspended and discharged within the high voltage of light waves transmitting in spiralling oscillation. These powerfully effective energies discharge higher vibrational bandings. The polarities are then positively re-activated by the superimposition of an higher energy which revitalizes them to original functioning.

Being evenly distributed at centralizing point, this new energy is being fed into the surface of the earth via the existing network of the ley line system. This intricate network resembling veins or capillaries has the capacity to absorb copious Cosmic energy which maintains and contributes towards overall planetary stability.

We want you to know that at present Earth is being succoured by those of us who have chosen to come to its assistance. We are also aware that this is merely a temporary state of affairs which must be finally resolved. Release of heart essence or love is now more than ever urgently necessary in order to disperse huge clouds of planetary darkness which if increased will mean death to Earth. We shall assist you at this time fulfilling our role of guardian to Earth. Many ascended souls stand with us, aware of a growing responsibility towards this particular and extraordinary service. These souls having chosen this incarnatory experiencing will remain upon Earth for as long as it is expedient to do so. They will not return until all witnesses completion. We join to them as soul kin.

Many will see us as translucent and bright beings. We move always as pure transparencies of Cosmic light having dimension and substance within the rainbowed spectrum. We are the first Creative Breath, the issue of all Create and Uncreate matter. Our permanent abode lies within the single eye of the Logos whose visioning we are.
5th March 1994

Precognition or foreknowledge is to be given to certain souls who will be required to act upon the content of specific information granted to them at requisite times. This preternatural gift is bestowed upon man as a fifth dimensional faculty or gift. Many souls will have undertaken this charge or task within other incarnations. They have been allowed to retain this faculty by deliberate choice, and throughout all planetary cycles. Now many other souls are being prepared to fulfil similar channelling roles. In time an ability to receive Cosmic signals will extend to all awakened souls, finding easy entry through the new brain bifurcation.

There may be initial confusion for many souls previously unaccustomed to the reception of this new signalling. Even when admitted freely, there will be conflicting thought following the inception of new concepts, especially when these support to new patterning inherent in future action. All signals depart from present acceptable norms and learnt behavioural traits. As the brain acknowledges the existence and realization of the new mind link within responsive acceptance, synchronicity will emerge as mind thought prints into a new understanding those signals transmitted by alteration to existing energy frequencies.

The soul transmitting this information resembles a receiver which absorbs many different frequencies simultaneously. The ultimate fine tuning mechanism seeking to interpret incoming signals has the end result of processing information with new clarity. All stages are viewed as contributive. Information is to be clearly defined before being transmitted to others. The accuracy of any message lies entirely within the integrity of the receiver, whose given task it is to translate telepathic signals into words given and understood within the normal channels of communication.

Many souls have developed the Cosmic faculty of a "telepathic ear" which in listening interprets with the right hand brain; this part of the brain is predominantly receptive or intuitive with regard to this particular programming.

Signals are then passed through to the left brain hemisphere which eventually accepts them. Processing finally taking place, is finally dispensed through the normal channels of speech and writing.

Cosmic signals are being transmitted within stronger frequencies. Our role is to "make aware" those souls who are awakening. Therefore there is at all times a requirement to feed relevant information to souls at specific stages of their evolutionary growth. Within the channelled messages exists a "double charge". The words themselves transmit an energy which is recognisable only to those who have already received them in previous incarnations and now receive their impact at an awakened level. The messages will have been carried forward in time and contained within the sleeping part of the brain since the first dawn of time. Now they emerge to touch many souls with similar energy, triggering a powerful response within those who admit them in a spirit of truth and love. For some they cannot yield their energy, for a proportion of souls the chosen moment in evolutionary growth has not yet been realized. Ultimately all souls will come to this phase as all enter relevant points of entry.

All will pass in soul cycle through the eye of the Cosmic portal, some finally returning to Source, others finding themselves within different cycles and at other planetary levels. Man is now at the end of third dimensional time. He is required to go forward. Many souls are entering into the fifth dimension. This is commensurate with individual, evolutionary growth. Before portal entry is effected, there will be a period of great searching and doubt where many will be tested, some being eventually recalled. Only the soul centred in love may come to the realization of the great light.

Children, put away fear, we are surrounding you with immense love and light. Stretch out your hand, we will take you towards that place where all is seen within the wondrous light of the Cosmic Dawn. There you will dwell immortally, clothed in the shining raiment of bright soul-light.

7th March 1994

We hold you in loving regard. It would be unacceptable for us to impose new concepts without affording you the maximum courtesy by way of information. It is vitally important that you are given the opportunity to understand the transitional changes which are taking place around and within you. The channelled messages are given for your edification and comfort. We are sharing Cosmic wisdom with you, previously this has not distributed to those who are at third dimensional level.

This implies that we actively seek your acceptance of future events. The degree of understanding rests ultimately with each individual and is commensurate with acquired intelligence level. If a state of active resistance occurs, these could build towards negative blocking creating impedance in spiritual growth. Such resistance reinforces old DNA encoded patterning which is largely strengthened by the Ego, together with persistent programming towards self preservation. These must be cleared before ongoing spiritual progress is ensured.

However, we are aware that any degree of change without due understanding of its relevant part and significance in future mutational programming could convey an increased sense of isolation and separateness of the self, together with an incapacity to see change as the viable spiritual platform it is intended to be, promoting soul development. We hold you in great love and brotherly esteem as soul kin. It is because of this spiritual connectiveness we are directing maximum effort towards gaining your full understanding and co-operation. This will assist towards raising spiritual levels prior to subsequent entry into fifth dimensional consciousness.

Strengthening of inner vision is required before you are able to receive and transmit at the new Cosmic frequency. This mode of communication when firmly established will assist towards the easier absorption of new energies. It will also provide linkage to us, providing a viable network and drawing upon a common pool of knowledge to great advantage. This communication mode imparted at inner mind level facilitates to fast assimilation of Cosmic telepathic content.

Single unimpaired visioning is requisite, all future visioning taking place within the etheric. Present third dimensional vision provides you with the necessary mirroring for earth experiencing. Dependent upon what you see, the eye records to the brain, triggering mood swings of elation, despair, joy or sadness. You have learnt to interpret through the eye ongoing assessment and resulting re-action to environmental and emotional factors.

The inner vision remaining independent, lies outside the normal field of vision and is unaffected by its transience. It focuses within the soul, mirroring that which is eternally linked to the Source. Many souls receiving the faculty of full Cosmic vision may at first distrust and question its unique signalling Appearing within and not crossing into the normal field of vision, it emerges initially as intricate and coloured geometrical designs or bands of swirling brilliancy which merge into unprecedented colour and form. These opening, disclose Cosmic patterning and oscillating frequencies. In linking to this incoming vibrational energy, there is fine direction towards the higher mind where there will be met recognition and fast absorption. In time many will come to witness and experience this mode of visioning which is part of mutational change.

We ask you to accept information as a significant aid towards insightful understanding. Your right hand brain has always indicated acceptance, although your left hand brain remains within a present process of reasoned consideration and deliberation! The time is coming when both hemispheres uniting will come to a single state of harmonized Cosmic synchronization. This will be conveyed in full Cosmic awareness and enlightenment.

8th March 1994

Soul light comes from the spirit which is the fount and breath of the Creative Source. This quality of light is enhanced within subsequent incarnations where there has been loving aspiration and motivation towards spiritual development. The soul saturated by light ray increase, opens fully. Then by powerful attraction, it is drawn towards the multi coloured heart of love.

Light is the key opening to Cosmic dimensions and revealing the secret wisdom of the Logos to souls imbued with spiritual intention. This knowledge is then gloriously shewn to the initiated entering its Portals.

Light energy is the main composition of the future etheric body, being wholly representive of symbiotic ascension. Transcendence coupled to purification effects total transformation within emanations of highly actioned grace. Light frequencies igniting, inflame the soul towards blissful loving, covering all to transfigurational phase.

Those who are soul-awakened, desire to dwell only within the light of the Source. They have admitted to its pulsating empowerment within their hearts. Seeking further purification and soul refinement within the spiritual flame of its healing energies, they come to be finally held within the blissfulness of radiating light.

The eye of the soul allowed to witness with growing clarity that part of its nature which is eternal will survive all physical enjoinings. At a defined point within its evolutionary journey it will come to vision and with Cosmic enlightenment, that which is wholly conducive towards its immortality. Within this heightened state, all fear thresholds will be finally expelled, leaving only the certain expectation of that glorious future which shall be joyfully revealed following completion of soul experiencing.

The endless song of the soul is then sung, lovingly emmeshed and held within the Heart and pulse of Universal embryonic sound, which is its origin and final point of return.

8th March 1994

You have upon Earth at present the visitation and significant overlay of Angelic protection. This will afford you succour in times of great need which are to come before you. A section from each hierarchy is presently here in manifold form and vesturing. Angelic beings are Galactic in nature and origin. They have elected to descend to third dimensional Earth, whilst retaining qualities inherent within higher dimensional form. Clothed in the vesture of pure light, they are invisible to the human eye, except to those who enter into their radiant light frequencies.

Many souls are being actively nurtured by them during this critical phase of evolutionary journeying. They carry with them in visitational flight, that substance of pure light energy which being received and absorbed by man, strengthens and sustains. Within consciousness, the soul is nurtured, taking into its mouth that "spiritual manna" which is also its own substance and essential nature. Had this noble service not been rendered and so lovingly, many by now would have perished due to declining and dimishing soul- light levels.

It is this light of spirit which bonds in powerful connectiveness Earth and Heaven. A transparent cord binding angelic being and earth dweller together in corded light, is symbolic of existing contracts which both have undertaken to fulfil. As man ascends, the etheric cord is shortened, pulling him up as it were into higher dimensional levels. This is presently occupied by the Angelic archetype whose image he must ultimately portray.

Each soul will be defended in these days by two Higher Beings, one to the right the other on his left, man remaining as the central pivotal point within a Trinity of triangular composition and beauty. He assembles the whole by the third and completing part of the Cosmic hologram. This is seen within true perspective as he becomes enlightened, illuminated and filled with grace. Until there is full saturation of soul-light, he is unable to manifest visibly as a true spirit. When this process is completed there is an immediate and even distribution of grace to all activated energy systems occurring simultaneously and within stepped dimensional programming.

It is because the level of many souls has dropped below the norm for required spiritual growth that a nurturing programme has been sanctioned.. Man will be unaware at physical level of this sustenance or of its light ingestion and absorption. It is given for ongoing re-vitalization and contains spiritual substance which actively feeds the soul during periods of great need. Angelic beings have accepted this group task as a service to man who stands before them as true soul kin. Their saving intervention has come at a time when many souls will express lasting gratitude for this glorious giving.

10th March 1994

Praise ascending from every created being raises a sung anthem of endless joying. This begraces the face of the Creator who reflects all emitted matter and energy to be mirrored faultlessly within the beauty of His infinite gazing. From the mouth of Creation flow streams of purest light which birth themselves into trillion myriad forms and colouring, these pleasing to the Great Heart of the Logos.

For all energy remaining faithful to and reproducing its own kind in original structure and form, the Designer takes pleasure and delight for in this It witnesses the first true creative thought. This is nature within followed season witnessing in true perspective the mind of the Creator. The realm of nature remains true to its first prototype, since its energy, although lower than man's, is unsullied by base motive. Any mutational change has been created by man. We view with sadness this process of abnormal change which has until now served to increase man's desire for the control of natural forces as a means towards further monetary consideration.

His constant ravaging creates deep wounding, penetrating the heart of the planet. Unwarranted change within nature results in traumatic long term effects. Do you not hear the screaming of Earth as she cries out in pain? Nature must eventually seek release in a powerful force which will rebalance Earth although at the expense of man. This force until now is held in check. The forces of nature will eventually rebound against the prolonged programmes of misuse. Instead of guardians we have scavengers who misuse natural resources, by wanton and wasteful destruction.

The artificially contrived substitutes conceived by man to replace natural resources are unpleasing to the Universal Source since their vibratory level is unstable. They feed a high toxin level into the stratosphere. As we informed you in earlier channellings this in turn gives rise to heavy obscurities by off-loading further toxic clouding.

The neutralization necessary to disperse such voluminous charge must remain ineffective where man is concerned, since he is unable to control the natural elements, namely direction of wind flow, rainfall, sea level etc. Nature is now failing to clear these poisonous particles totally, due to massive increase in distribution and redistribution. Blown by wind and rain, they infiltrate into densely populated areas, joining to similar poisoned emissions. In unpopulated zones, this artificial waste decimates many areas where Nature has for millions of years, acted as a safety net or rebalancer. For example, the rain forests in many countries have seen partial if not total destruction.

It is clear that man is unable to put back into the earth that which he has taken. We do however see many souls attempting to save the planet from further devastation by the reseeding of its natural resources. Would that they were more in number! The points we put before you at the commencement of this channelling was that all began in perfect praise, beauty and balance. The Creator is ultimate perfection. Man cannot emulate the Creative process. What he aspires to produce without spiritual thought will be nothing more than a grossly infected species bearing little resemblance to original created form or structure.

12th March 1994

Many new energies will enter Earth this year. Some of these energies initially presenting as difficult to harness within third dimensional level. The new frequency patterning is conducive towards fifth dimension at entry. With this factor in mind, all presently combined vibrationary levels will be accelerated.

There will be a gradual emptying out at third dimensional phasing, replaced by the higher levelling of the fifth. This transitional phase will take place gradually, becoming ultimately acceptable to all. The wind of the spirit entering into the awakened heart of each soul, and strengthening it with higher energies, will transmit a flame of Cosmic fire, which will open all to receive greater refinement of the present sensory organs.

Now all begin to speak with wisdom and understanding. This transmits light energised as love essence. Empowered by Spirit, all come and are imbued with new insight and integrity. Man stands then within "the ground of knowing." This touching upon soul sighting of that hallowed ground which is a true reflection and perception of perfected Creativeness.

The tongue empowered will teach again the Ancient Wisdom which has slept until now within the silent recesses of the human mind. The new energies provide the key to a new dawning of spiritual unfoldment. The day of renewal is now powerfully advanced. Lying within the reach of man, it comes to teach its secret doctrine to all initiate souls. Conveying as a spiralling and oscillating centre, it draws all towards the vortex motion of Cosmic naturing.

The human ear opens now to the sound of the Galactic Universe, absorbing with sensitivity the symphony of time and timelessness contained in endless space, attuning with heightening sensitivity to the voice of the Uncreate which is pure Source orchestration, the enhanced range of the auditory system now extending far beyond present third dimensional frequencies.

All incoming energy frequencies find clear pronouncement within new acoustical receptivities which attune sensitively to an opening dimension.

The eyes whilst retaining required optimum sight within third dimensional structure, are now opening to a new visioning which is inward becoming focused solely upon soul-witnessing. The new energies re-inforce this single mode of vision which is multi dimensional giving easy access to the new Cosmic linkage. This will have a maximum bearing upon the future light body, permitting its extended faculties. The Cosmic eye will give accurate telepathic measurement into zones of dangerous excursion, implication or risk. Normal vision will be as at present, but with the addition of seership well beyond the present range level.

Touch will be extremely sensitive enabling discernment where rising levels of incoming energy are presently undisclosed. The body will ultimately function at advanced levels where great extremes and marked changes in heat and cold occur, this with the ability to withstand and tolerate new thresholds which will be in great excess of the normal climatic and present range.

All mutational change will be effected over the next few years. Body change is already taking place, although at imperceptible level. Gradually this will lead to more pronounced change coupled to incoming waves of new Cosmic energies. These enabling rapid acceleration and absorption of the new body fluids which are essential in the new programming. As energy levels rise and are consequently experienced there will be a proportionate increase in body lightness. This may lead to temporary disorientation and systemic imbalance initially, followed by eventual eveness and permanent stability.

Many souls are arising to fulfil important roles as interpreters and teachers, guiding others into ready acceptance of presently required mutational change.

16th March 1994

Earth, in acting as the symbolic Christ, has taken upon herself the sins of the world. She is saturated and defiled by the harsh residue man has unleashed upon her. In the last years of the 1990's there will be a great purification where she will seek to cleanse herself of the totality of every toxinous substance imposed upon her.

This will be shown in massive earth upheaval where gross pollution is causing planetary instability and imbalance. Earth in this process of cleansing and purification will lift out mans cancerous inseeding. This, surfacing from the ocean's floor and from the volcanic rock, will distribute widely, showing great wounds of hideous disfigurement.

Man will encounter misfortune within the final purification. All future growth will be halted until the dead wood is pruned and burnt. The forces of nature will be unleashed against man. Acting as the balancer, she will come to restore and retrieve her territories.

Man shall witness to her wrath in world disaster, the result and aftermath of his own impropriety, earthquake, pestilence flood and famine surely following, these standing as retributive where man reaps a fearsome vengeance

The negativity of man is accelerating, breeding as poisonous energy. This malformation of spirit represents in your time as the ominous Anti Christ. All is compressed within this dark negativity manifesting as war, famine, desolation, isolation and spiritual agony. This destructive energy must be dispersed before transfusive transformation takes place.

Every man fulfils the contract of the symbolic Christ, his life taking on significant meaning with the cycles of birth, life, death and resurrection. In all these phases, he appears as angel or devil. Salvation is dependent upon the response accruing from these actions and the quality of life issuing from that role. From this spiritual platform he may aspire or decline. Every action, good or evil affects others by the final outcome of its deed.

Man is visibly affected by gross irresponsibility. Now he will have to accept the consequences for programmes militating against planetary well being. His present conduct indicates lower standards and a downward trend which ultimately may result in a massive decimation of his own kind. Destruction to the natural world without which he cannot survive, must be halted. The point of no return has not yet been reached, although the doomsday clock ticks relentlessly towards that final phase where the despair of all nations shall be witnessed. Whilst man continues to abnegate spiritual responsibility, there exists nothing more than stagnation and death. Men of right spirit, we implore you to turn again, living within the climate of light and love.

17th March 1994

The breath of the soul creates the climate for transfiguration. In that realized phase, Earth becomes Heaven. Emanations of pure Source Energy are coupled and absorbed at spiritual levels, permeating all created matter to Cosmic Light. This is the final phase where all souls eventually revert to original centering. This is the resting place of the lion and the lamb, and as dual and complementary energies merge, they become fused into one single energy which enfolds both natures as one.

Man resting within his own centredness views all aspects of his being with dispassionate gazing. He is the dweller in the stars whose eyes open only to the Light which he has become and of which he is an integral part. Since he is able to share in the Divine naturing of the Source he desires to emulate a higher vibration, sharing in its heightened frequency, so that he is raised, participating in the multi dimensional visioning of the Logos Itself.

The resurrection of mankind consists in aspiring towards the greatest good. Awakened consciousness imparts Divine knowledge at maximum level, qualifying soul essence, by recognition of its given dwelling and abode within the veil of flesh.

Once man touches into his soul, he is tranformed, animated and illuminated. In this state he touches the desireless mind which covets nought save the loving of that Principal Energy which created it. Then he is in love with love itself which becoming as a bright fire, signals him to enter the purifying heat of its flame wherein Divine union is consummated. Then, absorbed and in great refinement of soul, he is re-created as light issuing forth as original Source energy. Being soul identified and named, he aspires to simulate nothing except the nature of the Beloved which is endlessly mirrored in praise and visioned in creative imaging.

In this state awakened man accedes to the seat of the Logos which is the culmination of soul centering.

<u>18th March 1994</u>

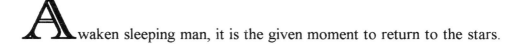Awaken sleeping man, it is the given moment to return to the stars.

For many millenniums you have slept since your deliverance was not given. Encased in earth matter you have lain within the vortex of time and until this age. You have remained where you fell at the dawn of Creation, when a lowered vibration of energy drove you from the Light of the Source. No eye then could bear to gaze upon your hapless state and we who remained have always wept and petitioned for your return.

We have worked since then for the regainment of your original state and spiritual energy. It is only within the realization of your true nature, that you will be allowed to return to this pristine state. The penalty you have incurred has been to sleep veiled in flesh, and without recognition of soul light. This has taken place over thousands of earth years and your light, formerly the brightness of the Cosmic Sun, has grown dim. The Karmic Earth has served to purify you, although this process has been slow covering many earth incarnations. Gradually your cycle of reparation is coming to its conclusion. All phases are now within final completion, touching termination at the end of third dimensional time.

Now it is given unto souls to see that glorious vista which has been closed to Earth sight. It is the glorious sun of the fifth dimension which is to dawn upon you with great light. Preceding this phase, there is yet awaiting you a necessary period of purification, this finally closes upon previously incurred penalties. You are to be restored and re-admitted to that Divine energy which marks you as children of the Source. We say to you that trust and confidence are the hall marks of this future phase. We surround you in great love bringing you to that former state which is your rightful inheritance. All which lies before you is as nothing compared to the ecstatic joy of return.

The natural law is dispensed within absolute justness. Since you fell from grace when you defied natural laws, your period of returning carries with it the rightful penalty of necessary purification. Imperfection cannot exist with Infinite perfectedness. All that you have inherited is the end result of former action. To return here you must be free from that which has lowered you to the experience of earth dwelling. You have paid a great price for your original disobedience. Separation from the Source, darkness, temporal abode, disease, sickness and finally death. All these are the purifying action of the Dark angel. You have undergone many earth cycles during your process of final purification. This knowledge has been hidden from you by Divine intervention, since we petitioned that this agony be witheld from you at conscious levels. Only the soul in moments of Union with the Source is permitted to recall its original state, this outside the physical and emotional bodies since these lower energy systems are unable to tolerate such knowledge without massive traumatic shock to the existing molecular structure.

Such knowledge given to you in love and trust, carries with it a growing sense of responsibility. This is to be discharged within the light of unconditional and loving service to all souls. Love is the redeeming energy which facilitates your return. Being entirely spiritual it finds easy access to the open heart of the Creative Thought. It is only within the fulfilment of this final contract that you may be finally re-admitted to the Light of the Source.

2Oth March 1994

We will come to purify the foundations of this house, for all that has been built upon her in time is as nothing." These words are given to Planet Earth by the Ascended Masters in the day of Earth dwellers sojourning 21.3.94. We carry the words of the Logos into every heart. These are carried upon the breath of the Universal winds. We amplify those energies which arise from your spiritual intentions. If the mouth praises whilst the heart remains closed, is it not barren and bereft of love?

Know that the action of love surpasses all, and that its perfumed essence spreads widely amongst spiritual men. You must come to recognise that Earth phases until now will be rendered empty and void if they fail to contribute towards the growth and emergence of spiritual identity and soul-wholeness. All else is a mirage, an illusion. Nothing ultimately has any permanence outside temporal time except the spiritual foundation for soul indwelling.

Children, your mouths are open to prophecy, your eyes to visioning. Upon your heads we pour the symbolic oil of annointment. You stand clothed in the vesture of holiness. We send you forth as messengers of the great peace. Those standing to witness Truth in the day of purification shall be sealed in light against the prevailing darkness which is closeted within the hearts of godless men. You will emerge in this prevailing darkness as beacons of light which are the pure emanations of soul energy. All shall come to you being brought to great comforting and healing.

Your feet stand within the portal gate, and your rightful entry into the fifth dimension is assured. Many who stand beside you will enter in fear. You in fulfilling the role of Saviour arise to redeem many souls, this by your petitioned intercession and love. The light upon your forehead represents the symbolic seal of protection. We have long nurtured you, preparing you in great love for the glorious day of transfiguration and ascension.

Your souls are open to us and their secret places known. We have illuminated you with the pure light of the Source and our gaze is always towards you.

Go then where you will, carried in and out of time by the wind of Universal Energy. Galaxies opening before you will disclose their Creative source. You will come to sit upon the throne of Kings. You are the precious seed of the Source, who will gather you to that final harvesting. You are become the air, the wind, the sun, the stars, all made resplendent within a glorious state of enlightenment. You are the pure flame which is the emitted energy of Universal Thought.

21st March 1994

It is within your inner space that we effectively communicate with you.

Your centredness is the inner sanctum wherein our messages are clearly audible. We are not to be found in the noise and turmoil of everyday life. Within this media we grow distant, our words unheard by men whose minds are open only to the materialistic. Go within, go within and discover your true being. Breathe in the air of the spirit.

The world in which you live and have being is greatly opposed to spiritual energy. It seeks now, more than ever to deny it existence. Those who are of the spirit realize that higher energies, due to their extensive vibrational charge may work effectively to neutralize and counteract the poisonous cloud gathering within the natural air you breathe. Because this is a preternatural faculty there are many who will not comprehend or subscribe towards these spiritually sustaining properties. This new energy is now inundating the Earth, literally sustaining life within souls who are moving towards Cosmic light inhalation. This gift of the spirit permits development of the deeper states of soul breathing The soul as the spiritual embodiment of life fulfils the role of affording refreshment to the physical and subtle bodies of man.

This energy is light contained within Cosmic composition. Its particles mix with the ascending air of a heavily polluted Earth, neutralizing and scattering copious streams of poisonous emissions. Those who recognise its pure essence are fed and nurtured by its transforming action. Many toxins are transmogrified by the action and input of Cosmic nutrients contained within this energy which is gently absorbed into the DNA, working to effect long term and positive mutational change. Your planet is being actively replenished by new energies. They signal to the purposed task played in future transitional programming.

Those souls who are not completely centred may have little time left or further opportunity to accept the new intake. Resistance to incoming Cosmic energy and its vital properties will gradually diminish normal lung capacity, resulting in a weakened systemic structure. By continued intake of present lethal concoctions which are the residue of waste, they will derive the minimum by way of required oxygen content.

It is within a newly formed and spiritual respiratory tract that prepared souls will be sustained by a purified air stream with inducement towards comfortable interchange. The new respiratory system will contain four new filters to draw off the volume of air borne gases and pollution which presently are giving rise to heavy ingestion and imbalance within the physical. With Cosmically refined and purified air, there will be a corresponding lightness conducive towards deeper breath inhalation. This will promote greater well being affording an increase of immunity against virulent attack by many new bacterial organisms. These will be deflected by the new protective system.(See previous channelling referring to the Light body.)

22nd March 1994

It is within the first moments of creative light that the soul emerges from its embryonic sheath, the time of birthing coinciding with the Original Thought Who breathes it into heightened spiritual energy. Joined to Galactic sources, and gathering from their naturing that intention which aligns it to Universal energy, it chooses to simulate the form and nature into which it is immortally spun. Spiralling, oscillating and rejoicing in its pristine state, it develops into a living representation of Creative Perfectedness. Carried upon the symphony of Cosmic sound frequencies and finally condescending to planetary levelling it takes temporary abode within the fragile housing of incarnate man. From flesh it continues to signal to the Logos, rendering endless praise and homage.

Soul composition consists of intricate and highly sensitized fibres of Source spiritually charged energy. These fibres, colour resplendent, contain the light of the Cosmic spectrum. The soul is nurtured within fused original energy which is unique, differing from all other energy forms. It carries an identity which is known only to the Universal network of souls. Communicating with the Source within individual frequencies and emissions, it is gifted to man within incarnatory cycles. Soul nature cannot be substituted emulated or simulated and is unable to return to Source until the final completion of its soul task. Its light, colour banding and soul grouping are known only to its Originator. It may refer only to that point of connectedness, admitting no other.

The soul rests by choice within the individual whose evolutionary path at lower planetary level it constantly seeks to elevate. Goals lie within an upward movement which is conducive towards spiritual growth and development. This evolvement is effected within incarnatory cycles. The soul, aspiring towards this spiritual zenith, ascends within the physical container; tranfusing its light throughout the earth body as it does so, it is raised to proper status by the ongoing recognition of its true identity and divine nature. As the human heart is purposefully directed by this soul-energy, it is illuminated and wholly saturated by Divine loving.

The soul assuming its rightful place as governor and ruler, operates between Galactic levels by directing powerful frequencies of soul-light energy towards the Source. This energy which is absorbed as soul essence, returns to enrich Creative thought.

23rd March 1994

The harness of the soul are the reins of Cosmic Light which are held within the eternal moment of Universal purposing. The soul is continually guided, fed and upheld by Cosmic indwelling. It is within this elevation that the soul emerges witnessing the magnificence of Creative Thought. This vision is deposited so powerfully within the soul that it witnesses only that reflection of the Absolute in which it is completely engrossed.

The soul being sealed to Source is resplendent within states of blissfulness which remain at constant level even when function is at lower vibratory oscillation. This Cosmic mindfulness enables the soul to maintain strong connectiveness to the Creative thought in all subsequent experiencing. Since its vibrationary level surpasses that of all other energy, it is enabled to transcend to the point of supreme elevation, remaining Source positioned and nurtured in earth incarnations. In this state it remains attached to the Source although it has the capacity to dwell within man at different level, and that simultaneously!

The task of the soul is to elevate itself within the physical structuring. It experiences within the framework of flesh, redirecting all completed experience towards the Source, there to be processed at Divine level. In this capacity it fulfils its primary purpose which is to elevate expression within variable spiritual frequencies. Although it remains indwelling within man, it may re-route to other dimensions within the Galactic whole. It is able to transmit spiritual energy or essence from or to the physical whilst remaining at   physically unmanifested level.

The exact seat of the souls indwelling will be shown to man at fifth dimensional level and beyond where it will presently manifest, functioning within conscious communicable signalling. Its future sighting will be determined by an evolved species who are able to witness its stronghold delighting in its given wisdom.

In third dimensional time, the soul directs and inspires man to go beyond the animalistic, its energy uplifting and nurturing. The composition of the soul and its purpose has been given within this channelling. This information is designed to aid man who now enters the threshold of a higher dimension. In fifth dimensional phasing, the body and soul of man will fuse in joyful union of Source return. The body of man transmuting to spiritual lightness will harness more pertinently to the high frequencies of Cosmic light which at present would prove intolerable to the existing system. The soul is preparing man for the advent of mutational change which is spiritual elevation.

24th March 1994

Soul maturity is established when spirit and matter combining glorify the Creative Thought within matched and balanced energy. Then great anthems of praise resound throughout the vaults of heaven, all magnifying and witnessing to the wondrous power of God indwelling within man who is the created manifestation of Source energy. Angelic beings, the purest and highest vibrational energy of the Uncreate, transport the returning soul within sight of its Creator, lovingly holding it within their hands and turning it to gaze fully upon that Divine Love which breathed it out as spirit. The hymn of praise is then ceaselessly sung by all peoples as nations pay homage to the Source for their redemption.

The Kingdom of the soul dwells within flesh, its seat discovered and discerned! All heaven triumphantly rejoicing to say Amen, Amen to the Creative Thought! Praise to the Uncreate who is and was and always shall be! Trumpets sounding loud the Cosmic note of joyous return and re-entry! All heaven listening to the powerful petition of mans ascending thought!

Not one soul is lost, all shall ultimately come to dwell within the light of the Cosmic Sun. That which is Created and clothed in flesh will be uplifted in glory. All partaking of Divine life shining as precious jewels, manifesting in light and witnessing the new Heaven upon Earth. What is stored for man is the knowledge of that Kingdom within the expression of Divine love, this given with open and loving hand. You shall receive its benisons, your hearts dwelling within its rainbowed spectrum. You are beloved Children of the Father upheld and gathered into the glorious dimensions of Light.

The purpose of the soul is manifest. It illuminates, actioning the elevation of Flesh. By Sanctification and purification of the physical, it guides, admitting towards the increased recognition of Divine energy, by disclosing its secrets to the initiate who walking within its light path comes to desire no other. The soul in loving hope bends towards the Source that nature in man which is Divine. The Creative Thought in raising the creature to spiritual form, seeks to reclaim that Original Source energy which is part of its own by the nature of redemption. The returning soul refined and enriched by its temporary abode within man finally re- unites with the Source as higher vibrational energy.

Man is the fashioning of Divine love. Within this energy he manifests, and without its increase during life cycles he cannot transcend to the higher consciousness which is his future flowering. The seed in man is the soul growing to fruition, nurtured and sustained throughout by Source energy, in full maturity ascending to spiritual capacity and within its chosen separation at Earth incarnation level.. The soul signalling endlessly to this higher energy, seeks constantly to elevate the physical counterpart until spirit and manifest matter rest in complete harmony and balance therein.
26th March 1994

The new energies contain cosmically encoded colour and vibration. These resonating frequencies are bestowed upon man enabling him to achieve greater balance and spiritual enhancement within the new dimension. A range of colours lying outside the third dimensional and normal mode of visioning are interpreted entirely within the subconscious, their heightened vibration giving fifth dimensional experiencing.

Imagery within inner spiritual states and stemming from meditational practice express powerfully towards formulation of symbolic and universal figuration. The strong pictorial content presented in this mode is highly significant of altered experience. Rejection of new imagery may be initially experienced by the mind. However the subconscious will subsequently open towards full acceptance of that which it has always known as conducive towards full development of Cosmic and spiritual consciousness.

Fear acts as an inhibitor, recalling more favourably former acceptable norms of behaviour. This is part of a re-assessment process seeking reassurement by conveying to the brain known practised and conventional modes. This will obstruct new energy input by effectively blocking it. New images are transmitted to the brain in altered form and new structuring. Many of your abstract painters have broken through this barrier, moving away from conventional artistry towards the practice of inner visioning. Then the eye of the beholder refocused, sees clearly from within. Gradually inception comes more consistently within that point of reference. Man stultifies from his desire to present as acceptable, conforming doggedly to norms of socially set behavioural patterns. Sight fixed at this outer level, merely re-inforces a conditioned response which induces replicated photo-mirroring confined to third dimensional performance

Part of the new Cosmic faculties will show departure from previous modes of visioning. The dream state where hypnogogic imagery is activated will show powerful departure from normal mind imagery, by-passing these with strong symbolic inflooding which may appear initially disturbing to the recipient. The Cosmic mode of visioning will in time stabilize affording comfortable insight into the fifth dimension which is called "the enlightener." Communication in this mode will by then be largely telepathic with imagery linking to Galactic sources and covering distance by mind thought as opposed to physical sighting.

It is therefore of vital importance that man should open his mind confidently towards the new energies allowing them maximum input. Once fear is dispensed with there will be an easy transition from present to future phasing. Our communication with man must increase enabling him to make maximum use of imparted knowledge by conveying new skills, this serving as ongoing protection from many dangers inherent in a future age of advanced technology and scheming artificial intelligence.

Man is growing away from the supported dependency of past idols! No longer does he require to emulate those qualities he sees in others. Rather he seeks to discover within himself spiritual qualities and those unrequiring duplication. His capacity is then extended to a new realization when he is powerfully aware that all he sought in this direction now lies within his own empowerment and centredness. Then he touches into the gift of spiritual discernment and awareness.

27th March 1994

57

The use of Cosmic numerals was given in earlier channelling. The new dimension will contain given numbers which are harnessed to particular energies. Certain numbers indicate the frequency range of a specific transmission. These numbers may be seen visually or sounded audibly within the mind at conscious level. The number should be received in openness of mind and retained for future referencing. All numbers carry the vibration and charge of the new Cosmic energies. Acting as carriers they discharge an electrical forcefield.

If a certain number is given this is indicative of Cosmic programming which is transmitted at that given frequency. For instance, the use of the numeral nine is concerned with evolutionary growth and when absorbed at subconscious or conscious level amplifies its resonance and energy by mimicking the shape of the numeral. When this figurative numerology is absorbed, an increase in spiritual expansiveness will present.

The number given in symbolic figuring represents the total sum of required energy input. Numerals generally will not exceed the single figure. If additional boostering to a specific energy becomes expedient, the shape of the number may be experienced as working within. Some souls may carry a given numeral within their visual field for several days. This manifests until total absorption is complete. This procedure will be within acceptable levels. We have explained changes to the visual field at fifth dimensional entry within the previous channelling.

The colouring of the numeral carries the essence of that particular energy. Nine supports high spiritual frequencies and is ingested as mauve or lilac. The colour banding may be in unspecified colouring, or outside normal visioning, this implies that the particular numeral contains the full Cosmic spectrum which has invisible banding. When white is relayed as the main ingredient, it will appear colourless to existing soul light being of similar composition.

It is important to understand the function of Cosmically relayed numerals. They assist towards the ingestion of new energies and are recognizable to the conscious mind as familiar figuring. Standing in your time as a new Cosmic faculty, their coded inception plays a vital part in mutational change which in adapting to energy assimilation gives access to higher levels.

Breathe the numeral in by linking to its vibrational frequency. Retain this for as long as is tolerable, then release by breathing out. If energy input falls below the requisite level, the numeral will manifest until energy transmission is fully effected, finally merging within the subconscious mind where it is retained at concealed level.

28th March 1994

To touch into the highest energy of all is to touch the face of the Source. White light suspended above all created matter forms into a protective and transparent layer acting as a protective barrier. It is not given to descended matter to pierce the veil of The Absolute, nevertheless all returning and ascending energy must be repurified to its highest spiritual frequency. Angelic beings shield their faces when in adoration before the Source. One fraction of a second in gazing and covering one billion trillion years of momentary sight suffices. Lower energy forms are programmed towards their highest evolutionary point. However they may not be admitted beyond the veil which contains the vibrancy of the Uncreate. However, gazing within sight of the veil threshold is sufficient for spiritual absorption and transformation.

The Logos being the pure essence of Divine love manifests to souls by condescension of Source energy stepped down to lowered levels. When this is actioned, there is perfected power and energy met within the higher states of super consciousness.

This is the holy ground upon which tranformative structure comes to admit and reflect the Absolute Light. The soul is the connector bridging the two natures of man, namely matter and spirit. It is composed of a tiny particle of Source energy, seeking always to effect permanent return. As we have set out for you in previous channelling, it achieves this programming by spiritual elevation

What is emitted carries purposed return. The circular movement of Creation is directional and representative of Universal energies which spiral ceaselessly backwards and forwards from their point of origin. Divine nature rests within that which is divine. Ascending upwards such energy seeks out compatibility and resonance within similar bandings of returning energy. Primarily cradled within the heartbeat of love it seeks reunion with that which birthing it, breathed it to form and structuring.

We stand within the light of the Source. We effect a double movement in momentary gazing. This action is both protective and necessary for those of us who have chosen to stand within your earth time. We are empowered to look towards both directions simultaneously; as we do so, our gaze absorbs from the Source a powerful charge of energy. We receive this, redirecting its power towards you. This bespeaks an action of great lovingness without which your returning journey would be long delayed. When we effectively look away from the Source we are able to do so in great joy because love balances our sadness even within momentary Source separation. We retain complete and continual gazing at all times. When we behold in you that awakened spark of divine nature, it comes to realize the pure reflection of Absolute light. When that divine spark grows to flame, we shall be as one soul one light.

30th March 1994

60

You are now entering into changes triggering great acceleration and vibration. These promote and link to the telepathic mind link which is a fifth dimensional faculty. The high frequencies contained in telepathic signalling travel faster than light waves, not only moving forwards but backwards and in circular cycle. In this state there will be a faculty of conscious precognition, giving indication of events outside normal time function.

This may occur within dream states or at conscious waking levels. There will be a merging and an ongoing link between reality and dream sequences. The ability to recall dreams clearly by harnessing them to conscious states will be utilized in programmes which teach and prepare for mutable change. The intuitive brain, partially asleep has at present formed minuscule links with spiritual experience. The memory banks of the psyche and the subconscious now opening, disclose the greater significance of dreams which, when accurately recalled at conscious levels, lead to degrees of insight within.

For many souls dreams act as balancers, aligning what man registers at inner level and is unable to express outwardly within acceptable social behaviour. Ongoing conflict or stress is resolved by the psyche during sleep and within dream states. However, in expressing of the new honesty, such processing will be unnecessary, since man in clear communication with truth will express his true nature. There will be an increase of spiritual inclination leading to effective communication with the subconscious mind. The subconscious is the "sleeping servant." When awakened it promotes appropriate insightfulness, raising man to his highest spiritual point.

If we were to tell you that sleep in the future will be at changed sensory input and that a continuum of consciousness would link into both harmoniously, it would be difficult for you to imagine the outcome! Awakened man will touch into dream sleep for the purpose of inner visioning. This will activate the subconscious to release interpretation within fifth dimensional experiencing. Body shut down will be activated by a different part of the brain so that sleep will cease to present the dream sequence as presently experienced. Future man will not require hours of sleep to revitalize the physical body. There will be an adaptation to lighter energies presenting as elevated etheric composition, brief moments then sufficing for present modes of long resting. As the sleeping brain awakens, man will learn to conserve energy whilst remaining in an awakened state, this without fatigue, or the previous requirements of general body "shut down."

At this time there will be tremendous emotional release, resulting in purification which will give appropriate alignment to genetically encoded and eroded DNA, this affording necessary correction. Finalized mutation witnesses to man who, evolving within the subtle and etheric bodies, exists within these at higher dimensional level.

4th April 1994

The iridescent eye rainbowing saviours to the eye of the Source. All light being held within its bright gazing covers by Cosmic thought the creative energy of emitted form and life. Loving vigilance overlays the radiant light of the Cosmos within whose pure brilliance and spectrumed rays dull matter is transformed into a spiritual fountainhead of resonating energy.

You are become that light and stand within the powering of its energizing rays. You are the coloured rainbows of the Divine Thought whose radiance permeates your souls. Each soul is a tiny spectrum of Source reflected light, reaching out to witness and praise the Creative Thought. You are that energy raised to the dignity of elevated divine intention.

Know that protection and love flows at every moment and within every heart beat aligning to and resonating with the Cosmic note. Your hearts beat as one in unison with all souls, one within the pulsating heart of the Source, rejoicing in sung magnificence of outpoured gracing. The Creative Being delighting in the souls of men, and manifesting as a loving Father, gathers into his opened heart the love of his children create. The quality of this creative love poured out upon man is unchangeable. He admitted to this glorious dimension is transformed, uplifted and elevated.

In spiritual ascent the soul glorifiying to the admittance of light witnesses to the Absolute Truth. This love opens every particle of energy to praise, and by doing so renders due homage to the Original Thought. Universes and galaxies are all covered by its energizing light. That light is the nucleus of the Source, activating and saturating all matter upwards and into super consciousness.

New energies carry powerful charges purporting to the increase of spiritual content. By re-enforcement, the awakening soul forges greater connectiveness to the Source by linking to dialogue at that entry point. Then opening to this new teaching, it is consequently drawn towards higher states of spiritual growth and, by single minded intention, attracted to a spiritual pathway, preferring no other.

The soul actively connected to the Source is replenished by spiritual light which is energy in its purest form. In this re-charged state it is constantly breathed in and exhaled from the Creative Breath which in the act of final inhalation, wholly consummates and transforms it to Cosmic light by a divine act of inbreathing in which it transcends to levels of absorption and Divine inclusion.

8th April 1994

The flower sheds its fragrance to all within its path, sharing its perfume with those who inhale its scented heart. Its main purpose is both single and selfless. It grows in perfected order and within due season to delight man and to beautify the Planet. Lying upon the breast of Earth and taking from her bounty that sustenance which is required in order to flower and fructify. This seasonal act of Nature satisfies the perfected law, ordered within cycles of growth, flowering, fruition and seeding. The final phase is earth sleep, where all is held within a dormant state. Then in rooted stability a new foundation for future growth is assured.

Man is the flower, his essence perfuming the ground of his being. The essence of the soul is symbolic of opened spiritual flowering. The soul, absorbing the rays of the Cosmic Sun, grows towards the Light. Then the petalled heart opens wide receiving powerful life force. Man is rooted deeply within the spiritual ground of Divine desiring.

He touches heaven when he aspires towards soul movement. It is within that climate that he grows into that part of his nature begraced by Source essence. It is only within this energy that he becomes both aware and enlightened. This is his flowering and fruition.

The seeding is when man is drawn towards the centre of the Source. Then he is impregnated by the single desire to fructify spiritual actions within further incarnatory cycles and by contracts of unconditional love and service. Selfless desire here reaches the maximum. There is then only the single desire to unite with the Beloved. This generosity of spirit voluntarily embraces all pain experienced in temporary separation from the Source. By acts of love and service the soul returns to Source, enriched and laden with new fruits of earth experiencing which delight the heart of the Creator. This is the expressioned anthem of praise which sounded brings angels to their knees in ceaseless adoration and homage. In that moment the creature is greater by an act of unconditional love than all other emitted and created beings.

The destiny of man is to flower and fructify, seeding in unending cycles of spiritual growth. He falls from heaven like a star to scent the earth. When that fragrance is emitted, all heaven is coloured by soul perfume. It is within this spiritual flowering, man comes to realize his finest hour.

Now comes in great array the vast army of just souls, falling upon the parched earth as a long awaited shower, spreading thickly upon the ground as scented flowers in full season. May their perfume spread widely.

11th April 1994

Y ou must look towards spiritual horizons since sensory experience, presenting as an illusion, will be unable to advance you towards that openness of mind which seeks only that conducive towards soul enhancement. You have come far and beyond all your previous expectations. It is your own limitations which have so far held you back. All is moving away from you at present with accelerated speed and light. You are moving in soul essence towards elevated states of Cosmic awareness together with an increased desire to experience those dimensions. That incorporated within you now exceeds all past experience. You are moving within your own centredness towards a new world which visions you powerfully to walk in the light and truth of the Source.

For this moment you took on the guise of flesh, for this moment you awaited the incoming of Divine Grace which is now abundantly outpoured. This is the hour of salvation, this is the time of returning. You are filled with the joy and wonder of new Universes unfolding before you, clear and wondrous is the light breathed into and through you. You touch infinite horizons, witnessing and touching upon your soul. Praise is your name! You are uplifted and restored to former celestial brightness! All is seen as undulating waves of sound, colour and energy. Recognising and beholding the glory of elevated creaturing, you come to witness the elevation of matter held timelessly within the great heart beat of the Uncreate. You are that energy which, clothed as immortal essence, is Divine outbreathing.

Much is given to you, much required, as the spirit rooted deeply within you continues to make powerful connection to the original energy which created it. You exist in Universal space, a soul complete within itself, spiritually functioning within the structured and contained flow of balanced energy and light. You are joined to that integral part of the great Universal whole which is the Galactic web of all living matter.

You are part of this great resurgence and tide. All matter eventually reaching and attaining perfected flow and resonance, mingles ultimately with pure Source emanation. Then only that spiritual remnant remains, in a greatly refined and purified state, this sanctified towards the Divine expressiveness. All contained within the Logos, is retained intactly and without denigration to eventually form an immortal part of the One original energy, which being fashioned by the Uncreate Mind originally emanated as a comparable, equable and Divine soul essence. What was emitted must purposefully return to Source. Such is your glorious destiny and final destination.

13th April 1994

P lanetary maturation occurs when both man and nature reach simultaneous ecological and spiritual evolvement. Each planetary system remains imprinted by genetic memory and within the cellular structure. The encodement of purified DNA now serves as an unconscious reminder towards increased spiritual maturation. Since man is unrequired to work within the medium of light space, a gravitational Earth base has been given where he may be birthed to life, grow and eventually age, ultimately suffering death and subsequent re-birth. It is within these cycles that spiritual maturation occurs. Where there is a sustained programme for ongoing, healthy spiritual growth, the original blueprint for man and nature is stayed within complete balance. This lies within the natural cycle and season. When there is dysfunction and interruption to spiritual phasing, abnormalities occur. If there is no reversion to healthy pattern, then normal phasing in maturation is replaced by malignancy and deformation.

This spiritual cancer gives rise to disease and premature death at all levels. Abnormalities noted both in man and nature occur as irregularities within the cellular structure, being shown as unfavourable growth. The ensuing sterility of man matches to sterility in nature since both are sustained by a common energy. Where there is death to nature, death to man inevitably follows. Man and nature are commonly bonded by the Universal law of cause and effect. Man existing within a favourable environment and discharging soul light draws upon himself a positive charge by culling energy which is positively linked to pertinent spiritual charge. Many life cycles faced to the charge of negativity and disregard for the natural law, will reflect a bitter inheritance within DNA encodement.

It is when such malignant growth is evidenced, and planetary dysfunction takes place, that reversal towards healthy patterning fails and is subsequently negated. Then that planet is voided to Universal spacing having failed to achieve primary targeting and objective by disinclination towards ongoing spiritual perfectedness which has been given within allocated orbital and gravitational spacing. Your own planet shows irregular patterns of growth. These are noted with great concern by those of us who are appointed, and carry the responsibilities of Earth Guardianship.

Within your own Galaxy and those brought into physical view by the advantages of artificial scientific programming there exist many voided planets. All these at one time flourished with teeming life in fruitful and ordered cycle. Their occupants susceptibly weakened by lowered infiltrative energy, gradually succumbed to patterns of sterility and gross malfunction which affected DNA encoding. Life force weakened as nature failed to provide a stable and viable platform for survival. Distorted gravitational pull and excessive fluctuation of climatic conditions brought extinction to many planets on a massive scale. Finally the life force of the planet ebbed, eventually replaced by the inert force of dead heavy matter. Voided Planets remain in space as a reminder that Universal Laws must be scrupulously observed. The penalty is a continuation of unfavourable conditions prohibiting future habitation.

Life on these malformed surfaces cannot be envisaged at any point, reversal is not possible. Voided Planets continue to pattern in space within distorted orbiting and unstable climatic condition, showing unsuitable habitation for man.

Planets ascending towards fulfilment and the completion of their spiritual contracting re-orbit at changed frequency. They claim inclusion into new dimensions which affords them enhanced spin. This permits them to enter Source energy zones which re-charge them to heightened evolutionary spiral as they reach towards spiritual planetary maturation.

Many of the voided planetary systems, some of them many light years away have been given over to lesser energies discharging unspiritual energy. If this energy is encountered by man, there will be total incompatibility and disorientation. Some of these energies may envelop present form with hologrammic disguise which mimics artificial intelligence. Many of these have attempted to invade earth in the hope that this planet, may at some future stage provide suitable housing for their indwelling and activities. So far they have been unsuccessful in their efforts to infiltrate, although their vibrational energy when experienced is indicative of total soulessness.

The light now shining out from the Earth predisposes towards wholeness, a spiritual reversal is taking place towards total Planetary healing. As man's light grows stronger we dare to hope that this Planet will survive the bitter onslaught of Godlessness. We call to men of right spirit to stand powerfully within the pure Light of the Cosmic Sun fashioned by the Uncreate Mind which is continually emanating comparable, equable Divine soul essence. What is emitted must purposefully return to Source. Such is your glorious destiny and final destination.

13th April 1994

It is within the clear vision of soul light that man comes into new understanding concerning his spiritual nature. This awareness prompted by the workings of Divine Grace lead him to experience fully fifth dimensional level. Man in harnessing the new faculty of soul-tuning may move towards higher states of consciousness. This Cosmic gift allows him to vision the soul accurately, witnessing its true state and present level of evolvement. Such visualization accompanied by powerful motivation, guides him to repudiate all that is unacceptable and outside spiritual advancement. There can be no vestige of despair at this phase, even though the figuring of the soul when seen, will carry the scars and blemishes of failed incarnatory experiencing. Man will be strongly motivated to work towards beneficial soul change, promoting realistic and spiritual growth patterns which are linked to ongoing cleansing and purification.

At fifth dimension entry, man is afforded the unique opportunity of soul witnessing. For many this may be a painful experience as they come to look upon their own soul with the growing realization that it is not without the penalties imposed upon it during earth dwelling. Spiritual abnegation conveys lowering energy to the fine structure of soul composition. This is sustained by man during life cycles, although damage may not be totally irreparable or permanent. As man grows towards spiritual refinement there is healing, this combining with greater sensitivity towards future soul-marking. An acute awareness of situations serving to diminish soul-light will be apparent. There will be motivation to work purposefully towards soul healing and a permanent state of restoration will be sought.

The soul at changed level, indicates that which is specifically required in the attainment of absolute perfectedness. Purification and release from past Karmic contracting frees the soul, aligning it more appropriately to spiritual easement. A new connectedness and bonding aligns man to reach his Cosmic pathway and destiny. In this phasing man chooses to place himself above materialistic values. realizing that these are obstacles which preclude spiritual advancement.

There is a necessity and ongoing need for accurate assessment and appropriate regulation of soul growth. With increasing spiritual desire, the inclination towards the development of soul tempering is requisite. Ability to vision the soul as one might scan the physical body is advantageous. With growing soul light nothing is hidden. The soul manifesting and shining through the physical body shows clearly to man. Looking upon the soul, indicates the level of evolvement attained, this is a necessary factor in re-admittance to Source. It is within this powerful hour of soul-searching that man now stands.

15th April 1994

The soul is like a bright star travelling to earth and birthing within the fabric of man. Once the soul assumes its habitat within dull flesh, there is clear indication of goals which in promised faith, finally transfigure matter into spiritual substance. However man may attempt to deny the existence of the soul within, he will at some divine moment come to experience its reality, purpose and indwelling.

In silent moments the soul impresses with such vibrancy that man may not ignore its powerful communication. No matter how often he closes towards its sensitive programming, by keeping watchful vigilance, it constantly re-charges the heart towards the opening of spiritual inclination by saturating it with love essence in which it is fragranced.

It is the loving receiver of all spiritual aspiration gathered inwardly within states of measureless faith. Resting within trust and confidence, it grows within the centre of man, opening him to love of which its heart beat is composed. The soul is more truly man than his physical counterpart, choosing to remain hidden within body density until finally radiating transparently through flesh, it manifests itself in the pure light in which it is clothed.

Since it is the embryo of the Source who deigns to dwell within incarnate flesh, it consequently owes allegiance to that Divine energy which created it and to which it will ultimately return. Within man it chooses to endure temporary separation from that Creative love which birthed it, and by loving volition, giving total commitment to earth body experience. The physical body of man is like the darkness of a tomb to the soul when compared to that light which, at Source level, faced it towards the bright rays of the Cosmic Sun. The memory of Divine light cannot be effaced by the soul who will constantly strive to regain spiritual height by working to advance the spiritual evolvement of man. This during its self imposed exilement so that Source separation may be concluded as the partnership of both body and soul enters into a new phase of enlightenment.

The soul is the overwhelming gift of the Source to earth man. Without its indwelling he would be nothing more than a chemical body whose existence would depend merely for physical sustenance upon signalled sensory input. The soul leads man to desire additional spiritual nurturing. The souls indwelling within the density of the physical man is indicative of the Divine promise of immortality, which gives man spiritual entry at higher dimensional levels. It is the promised task of the soul to dwell within flesh by elevating and harnessing man to his soul nature which is essentially Divine.

When the soul departs, there is immediate cessation of the physical. In what state the soul departs from the earth body, rests upon past experience which linking both physical and spiritual counterparts are wholly productive of and conducive towards Source return. If the soul by omission has failed to achieve spiritual goaling, it is by further assessment and deliberate choice, returned to achieve its objective within returning another physical body. This act of returning to incarnatory cycle deprives the soul of admitted Source contact and visioning, committing it to remain at lowered vibrational level until spiritual targeting is reached. Then there is realization of the ascended trinity of mind, body and spirit. Man is nothing more than his soul. The soul begins man to Eternity.

17th April 1994

76

There is much confusion at present amongst souls seeking their own guidance and spiritual path. Great proliferation of new content pertaining to the realization of spiritual development is growing. With its amassing there is increasing uncertainty as to what is appropriate or conducive towards spiritual growth. Younger souls appear to suffer from lack of purposeful direction and guidance where many spiritual teachers are concerned. There is strong evidence of an emerging superficial overtone in teachings which are without appropriate spiritual foundation.

The restlessness of the age attracts many souls to follow various schools of thought, some of them may dwarf and inhibit spiritual growth by leaving souls in complete dependency upon a particular leadership. Teachers are failing in spiritual responsibility towards these groupings if they encourage souls to follow dominant, charismatic leadership. This is indicative of a highly prevalent Ego especially if the leader with strong needs of his own, attracts by subtle influence, individual or group following. This is the seed sown upon stony ground which will wither away in the climate of testing change.

Souls are coming into an age where each may realize their own spirituality and Christ consciousness. Single paths should be favoured as opposed to the multiple which engenders little except fickle change and preference for an ever glamorous and transient scene. There are many false prophets and discernment must be used where dubious charismatic leaders are concerned who offer short cuts to spiritual development and growth, by extracting from the gullible, excessive monetary gain into the bargain!

The teacher who is prepared to give unconditionally, often without material reward is one whose main desire is to lead souls towards their own growth and centering. Everything is within, nothing is outside the self. Spiritual enhancement comes from within, emanating from the light of the awakened soul. Many admitted to the realization of spiritual inwardness will joyfully increase in spiritual desire.

Soul restriction is unproductive. Many souls need no more by way of spiritual direction than to be told to touch into their own centredness, peaceful and still, listening in silence to the note of the awakening soul. We have in the second channelling set out the naturing of the soul. This to be fully comprehended by those who follow a spiritual path.

With the growing recognition of soul kin at this phase, there is a strong tendency to establish and form groups whose main aim is identification by sought contact of those who are mutually attractive to others at group level. This often excludes souls, by reason of group and human selection, leading to rejection and isolation of those who are not socially viable. Ego orientated groups attract many younger and immature souls into regimes where they feel accepted and experience security. All are one soul, one light. With the passing of this particular phase, many souls will be drawn to follow more individual paths. Then they will grow towards awareness within individuality, realizing that personal growth which stems from their own centredness.

17th April 1994

The modus operandi with all new energies is to allow them to infiltrate slowly into the physical where they will discharge effectively. since Cosmic energies are air borne, maximum benefit is derived when inbreathed through the nose or mouth. Mingling with the necessary oxygen input and existing balance of body chemicals, they distribute evenly throughout the physical, heading a programme of mutable change. Overlaying the genetic structure, they have a propensity towards new growth, essential in fifth dimensional programme.

Of Cosmic composition, they lend readily to existing body temperature by clearing and raising organic structure. Their main effect is to lighten heavy genetic encumbrance. This clearance to physical matter is expedient in future climatic change, and eliminates the dead weight of former eroded DNA. encodement. Man will be required to literally rise above the contamination of a heavily polluted plant. Future climatic change will place him in grave danger should he fail to ascend to higher dimensional level, and in so doing, breathe safely into a purer air stream.

As we explained in earlier channelling, this will necessitate changes to the nose, throat and total respiratory system. These organs adapting to new expediency measure by the formation of an altered filtering system will give immunity against new strains of virus which will accompany world pollution. Infection is presently increasing, lowering the immune system to dangerous levels of overloading. There is an increased risk by way of chemical poisoning, which is readily secreted in the body by the rapid multiplication of micro-organisms which replicating within the host, defeat natural immunity and antidotes.

Abusement of the natural law incurs the greater penalty of transmitted disease which carries the maximum penalty for man. Powerful organisms invading body tissue and structure have disastrous potential for replication by their ease to multiply. These organisms are strongly resistant and heavily defended against curative treatment. They will give rise to widespread contamination leading to major epidemics, which will cause the decimation of millions.

Many souls now grossly infected, cannot adapt to the new energies since their bodies, racked with terminal disease, function at lowered and incapacitated level showing damaging viral infiltration beyond repair. The physical and subtle bodies suffering from deforming disease are incapable of the requirement of mutational change.

The awakening spirit of man is facing towards Cosmic enlightenment, conferred upon him by Universal evolutionary movement. This triggers Cosmic energy waves to make their way to your Planet. Do not fear them, rather receive them in a spirit of confidence and loving trust. They are an indication of a new spiritual future and dimension.

Given to Earth 20th April 1994

Man is unable to experience wholeness and balance until he opens to his spiritual naturing. Until that integral part of the soul is keyed, there is ongoing fragmentation within physical composition rendering him susceptible to superficial witnessing outwardly based and orientated. In this state he is vulnerable, an easy prey to illusory impression which draws him into a kaleidoscope of transitory pattern and change.

Recognition of the true self shows entry into the higher states of consciousness in which man remains permanently grounded, there is no separation at Source inception. Temporary time creates an illusion in thought patterning. Time frets and fragments, disconnecting the soul from prime energy which matches to the super consciousness. Time is an usurper often slowing motivation for spiritual change by ego saturated thoughts of despair or unmet goals, strongly reinforcing permanent loss and the expectation of deferred reward.

Some of you will be given the opportunity of experiencing two consecutive incarnations within the present existing body. This event cannot be reviewed in the light of present scientific knowledge, which must be dismissive and without spiritual insightfulness. Physical death actually taking place, will appear shortened, experienced within altered time shifts, physical cessation taking place within seconds. Complete absence of pain and fear will accompany this temporary separation of soul and body, conveying an overall sense of peacefulness. Those who have experience of this, may find it confusing and somewhat difficult to comprehend, wondering if the actual event ever took place! Be assured that it did so! The soul alone will be fully aware of the subsequent incarnation, which in linking to new spiritual pattern, enters higher thresholds in evolutionary journeying. This shortens the normal cycle within incarnatory experience, accelerating spiritual development to its maximum capacity, and eliminating the usual stages of maturational growth and development.

The former life is recalled in impersonal presentation, and reviewed without emotion. Although the memory banks retain the experience of the previous life cycle, there will be noticeable difficulties in recalling its significant events. The second incarnation covers the former, the latter being significantly charged and strongly empowered towards spiritual content. Motivation towards spiritual goals will be strongly evidenced within this subsequent cycle. Second lives within the same physical body are afforded to souls nearing completion in evolutionary phasing, and whose merits in love and service, exceed the normal. There is of course a deliberate choice by the soul to take on this subsequent incarnatory joining at the commencement of its penultimate phase.

22nd April 1994

Healing energy has a resonating flow which distributes in even wave

to the receiver. this force stems from a pure desire of the heart which transmits wholeness to all. Nothing impedes this stream of energy which flows in pure love tide towards those absorbing its life giving properties. Energy interchange permits healthy flow at physical, emotional and spiritual level. Contained within clear signalling aligning healing energy it attracts spiritual wholeness. The healer standing symbolically as the Cosmic Christ, embraces the whole world with outstretched arms. Healing energy, which is love essence encircling the world would restore all to planetary wholeness.

Every soul possesses the capacity to heal, although many souls believe that this is a gift given only to the chosen or privileged. The healer in releasing love essence balances unstable energy flow, magnetizing and re-aligning negative polarities in favour of positive ionization. If the energy waves sent out by the healer could be observed, they would have similarity to a re-charging electrical field, which is rapidly absorbed into the physical, mental and emotional bodies of the recipient. This flowing and resonating circuit resembles a continuous rainbow of spectrumed light, supercharging with maximum frequency, and replacing depleted energy with vital life force.

Since all are one and everything is connected, there are no divisions, man alone makes separation by seeking to divide. Energy or life force is peculiar to all men and is mutually interchangeable at thought level. It is important to realize that the positive thought of intention to heal possesses immense curative properties when transmitted by the mind. It is from this area that the healer will transmit a purer form of energy. When thought is directed towards, and held within the hands, there is dilution and at times, risk of contamination. The healer by directing hand contact, inevitably enters into the auric and etheric field of the patient and by attempting to redirect incompatible energy may become drained or even infected by the irregular instability of faulty energy flow.

Protection must always be sought by those who are involved in the healing ministry, although there should also exist a modicum of common sense! Energy lines running into other frequencies absorb and often take on their host naturing. If this were not so, then any healer's efforts to transmit energy would be abortive. They directly transmit their life force energies during the healing process. It follows then that the impaired energy of the sick also transmits, running to common energy lines and joining to the frequency of the healer. Although many will contend that they are cut off from negative ions they are, in fact, always open to them since there is a tranfusional flow where one energy is always dipping into the other. This process takes place through the action and efforts of the healer who counteracting depleted areas induces the patient's system towards healthier function and flow. There should be an awareness that healers should at all times draw upon Source energy which is inexhaustible, and that this energy and not their own, should be harnessed. This gives greater protection against imbalanced energy which could infiltrate into, and affect otherwise healthy vibrational flow.

24th April 1994

A PREFACE TO THE TEN PROPHECIES.

The ten prophecies are to be given at this time, in the hope that those who read them will discern their true spiritual significance The purpose of the messages are intended to convey a sense of urgency in working towards spiritual goals. They are not in any sense designed to engender negativity or fear, rather to enhance the opposite qualities of love and trust invested in positive hope for the long term future of man.

Many reading these messages may experience misgiving and natural fear. If the end result is clearly envisaged, all impending disaster is to be seen as a necessary purification process, and pertaining to the end result which is ultimate Source return. Perfectedness is only reached by the refinement of all which stands in opposition to that state. Man has incurred severe Karmic penalties, These have to be met and discharged. If this entails planetary disaster, then it is this phasing alone which will satisfy those Natural Laws which have been broken.

There is yet time to effect reparation. The note of hope running through all the channelling is one where mankind by raising spiritual levels is in a position to influence the final outcome. The necessary work rests always with man. He is the catalyst and his own Saviour. Of course there is Divine intervention and given assistance by higher beings who surround earth in great love and concern. Man needs to petition strongly for that degree of intervention, such cannot be given without his willing consent.

The prophecies are an indication of future events and not certainties. They are events which may be modified or even withheld if the Natural Law is satisfied by other processes. All depends upon the changing attitude of man and his response to the role of appropriate accountability and guardianship.

Because we believe that you who read into the possibilities of this forecasting are mature souls, we entrust to you the future of the Earth and the inevitable outcome. The Earth rest within your hands. What will you do with it?

May 6th. 1994

In the day when Atlantis shall arise from the sea standing as newly purified land, then shall there be witness to the Ascension of worlds and peoples. All being drawn into the vortex of time and space shall stand clothed in spirit and truth. The earth will be removed and spun into spiritual space revealing the secrets of hidden Universes and Galaxies. These will then come to form one undivided Whole. Time shall scatter its seed to the sky witnessing to the union of all emitted matter, which meeting fitly will be joined within one common structure. Then shall there be seen the fullness of earth, sea and sky manifesting to Universal completion and Divine overseeing.

The fruits of the kingdom shall replenish and satisfy the spirit, rekindling the earth to plentiful harvesting and in season. All witnessing to full visioning in spectrumed colour and light will express the Cosmic note, sung as pulsating silence contained within vibrationary sound. Light closing the eyes of the physical body will open then to the single focusing of the visionary. Praise resounding from the mouths of myriad souls, is carried upon the winds of the Cosmic breath, to rejoice and seal the newly birthed Universe to Divine inbreathing.

Moons and Suns shall process before the veil of the Uncreate Who may not be seen by man even in an evolved and spiritual form. Stars shall fall out from the heavens to rain upon the earth as bright hail. The shining light of these resetting the earth to spiritual time and signifying the completion of Karmic contracting. This day shall witness to the moving of Spirit; the sound of his wings will be heard, deafening to those who have resisted his noting. To the ears of the initiated this will be as sweet music and heightened vibrancy. All shall sing to the beauty of the Cosmic note which, reverberating from shore to shore, will amplify within singleness and purity of light wave frequencies. In that day sound matching to the speed of light will carry into new vibrationary wave.

Man will travel as light as the winds transversing the face of the earth. He will be as a winged form knowing no restriction and possessing boundless ability to communicate with all creation. Praise shall be in his mouth for evermore. In that day of enlightenment, he takes on pure spiritual form. Then he shall cast no shadow and his reflection shall not be seen. He will be as light itself, fully centred within the Cosmic sun, whose heat shall not burn or harm. Burnished brightness encircling his head, he will cast powerful rays upon the heads of unbelievers. One glance denoting pure singleness of eye which will draw all towards him in integrity and truth. As true son and heir, he is to be counted as glorified and blessed, standing as one who is fully admitted to the dimension of Cosmic light.

25th April 1994

In the day when the land mass suffers gross disturbance there will be a turbulence of great magnitude and force. Seas, rivers, mountains and hills, together with all assembled structure disintegrating, will be forced downwards by the powerful action of oceanic propulsion. The core of the earth arising will emerge above sea level. This linked to the tense heat of volcanic action, shall witness to the sight of the submerged ocean bed. Many new continents, arising from the seas will then be witnessed by surviving nations. The new land mass will take the place of many existing promontories. Those sinking beneath the rising waters, will remain contained at that level until such time as the penalties of existing Karmic contract are completed and sealed; this, even until the next phase of planetary upheaval. When the purification process is ended, all land masses will again re-emerge witnessing new spiritual transformation.

Gravitational pull will present as grossly displaced causing great instability. The axial plates will weaken, eventually disintegrating. In the final displacement, there will be detachment from these natural anchors which will occasion free fall into space as the planet veering and zig zagging attempts to restabilize, re-orbiting into new directional paths which may cause collision by its close proximity to other Galaxies. This is the ultimate effort on the part of the planet to recorrect itself by effectively detatching from accumulative disorder. With erratic change and unstable movement to both polarities, unseasonal climate and abnormal sea rise will be evidenced. Top heaviness in one or other of the planet's polarities will lead to a tilting of the earth causing rise of the sea level. Many continents and islands will become completely or partially submerged, lying beneath the great flow of accumulated water. Many will perish as these waters cover the greater part of the earth's surface.

For those who survive, there will be an intense period of suffering. Pestilence and scourging will be evidenced. Great fire plumes, the effects of massive volcanic eruption will mix with rising vapourizing water, creating dense fog which will darken the earth blotting out the light of the Sun. Dust particles accruing from volcanic action unable to disperse, and carried erratically by abnormal wind flow, will act as a shield and barrier failing to allow for the even distribution of heat, and leading to colder climatic conditions where nothing grows upon the earth.

Man will eat like an animal from the withered grasses of the field competing with the birds of the air for scarce sustenance. His abode shall be as at the early dawn of time, open to the elements and unsheltered. He shall face the unleashed forces of nature with fear, reminiscent of his early ancestry. Nothing of the social order will remain, all learning and skills will be obsolete and useless.Man will come again to survival with crude and primitive skills. There will be chaos and great upheaval. In those days he shall reap his own bitter harvest. The only viable platform will be the spiritual, when he shall petition his Creator for deliverance. Then he shall be heard, for there will be seen, the foundation of a heaven upon earth. Man working in partnership and harmony with nature, will by loving intent create a spiritual paradise where heaven touches new earth in fruitful plenitude.

The time of the great division shall witness those who stand within the light and those who have chosen paths of darkness. Grace shall be withheld during this phase to those souls who have failed to clothe the spirit in love. Because of an impoverished soul state, they shall not enter into the Cosmic portal until the second and final Cosmic note is heard. They shall remain outside this gate in great sorrow and tribulation until they are fired by spiritual desire to be admitted and reclothed within light. Then reclamation taking place, they also will be admitted during the final phasing.

Those who have stored spiritual energy, shall have recourse to such in times of great trial. They will witness the powerfulness of its light. It shall burn brightly within the heart of man showing him into ways of truth.. There shall be joyful walking within this light which will show to safety in times of great darkness. It shall encompass the man whose spirit is joined to that of Angelic beings. These walking before him, shall clear all dangerous paths, ushering that soul to spiritual solace and refreshment. He shall travel towards the holy hill, resting therein.

The body clad in the vesture of light, rises above all heavy encumbrance. It travels as the wind, rising far above the earth and avoiding zones of danger. It shall remove to an oasis of greenness and peaceful dwelling which is a chosen and fitting place for the habitat of the soul. From such protection man may safely dwell in love, directing purposeful lazer rays of focused thought to souls in great distress and dire need. This mind energy travelling faster than the speed of light and swiftly reaching its destination is powerfully emitted by the mind. Its frequencies searching and scanning seek contact with the receiver, who absorbing its life force is re-invigorated by its energy. This mental antenna tunes into, and scans zones of depletion by the use of the Cosmic mind link. The link attached to the light body is activated and transmitted by the energy wave of the third or single eye, giving full comprehension and seeing.

This is a Cosmic faculty given to souls who have attained spiritual evolvement, and will assist many benefiting from its healing ministry. It is emitted from the soul-light of Earth Guardians." The guardian is a soul who has chosen to protect and guide earth and its inhabitants during times of great crisis.

Many will cry to be heard and shall not. Many will be succoured and made safe. This will be manifested in the day of great division when just and unjust souls are finally separated. The souls of the just will enter, petitioning endlessly for all who remain outside the Cosmic portal. They will make great intercession as those standing in darkness and in great sorrowing. The bowels of the earth shall come to swallow them as it swallows the land. After many years of purification, they will see deliverance ultimately tranformed into light by the spiritual ministry and intercession of ascended souls. All shall finally enter into the Cosmic portal. Then shall the shout of Praise reverberate throughout the heavens as nations pay due Homage to the Logos who is the Source and Being of all created matter in time and space.

28th April 1994

The heavens opening will disclose celestial fire which shall penetrate the earth as tongues of flame. The flame signifying the symbolic configuration of the Logos- Source- Uncreate, appearing as even and triangular in shape, having apex and base with three sides. All men who are sealed with this sign shall have protection. The symbol of Cosmic indwelling will be seen, imprinted upon their foreheads. Light issuing from this sacred symbol far exceeds the light of the sun, which is seen as a mere shadow by comparison.

Those who receive this symbol shall gain access to fifth dimensional overshadowing, conducting men towards new teaching which is given at inner level and without the requirement of reading.

Written material by this time will be almost non existent, books, will be scarce. Mental telepathy will convey by direct communication, requisite and necessary information. This will be relayed by the medium of light waves which pool spontaneously into the main grid having access to past, present and future knowledge. Knowledge having been stored for release at an especial time, is given to those awakening to newness of spirit. Information concerning present and future global change will be given in this way, channelled through the new brain bifurcation, described in earlier channelling. With the input of supplied data and programming, it will be possible for future man to adapt to massive change engendered by planetary disaster. Such changes requiring swift absorption in the use of new skills.

The new age will abhor the use of artificial intelligence. The natural skill of man will be called into use by a primary need to create order out of chaotic world conditions, these skills setting new standards. Technology which has promulgated and incubated deformative robotic energy will be useless to man. Although there may be sporadic attempts to revive this intelligence by men whose eye is darkened, there will be growing evidence of it's malfunction, leading to eventual blocking of its intent and purpose.

In sites where atomic energy has been previously used, these have grossly affected those living within its shadow. In these areas there will be nothing left except barren waste land which forfeiting natural energy, will lie inactive for thousands of years. Gross earth contamination has occurred in these debased areas. Total purification may not see completion until many ages have passed. This is the natural law of cause and effect.

Advanced technology will be useless to man in the light of world wide planetary disaster. There will be no chance of making ready space vehicles or of effecting a speedy exit to other Galaxies. When doomsday strikes, the impact to Earth will be sudden and swift, finalized in minutes. Remaining man will revert to a primitive mode of life, required to access new working relationships, namely those bringing him into a closer partnership with Nature.

This opening him to Cosmic consciousness as he re-embraces the truths of the Ancient Wisdom. Man post Armageddon will be essentially a man of peace, his nature harnessed to that which confirms this quality. The sign of the Cosmos sealed upon his forehead, stands for the Divine promising, elevating souls who walk within its light.

29th April 1994

When the Cosmos reaches saturation point, there will be expulsion. The delicate balance of gravity will be affected and overloading will have the requirement to shed that which has given rise to unfavourable condition. Such climate inclines the adroitness of the planet to gross instability, which may not be redressed. Even with effected counterbalance the ensuing results coming too late will be fatal. A drifting Universe will be at the mercy of other planetary systems having dire consequence. Pieces of planetary fabric dislodging and effecting free fall, will in space become inert matter, forming debris and causing obstruction to the remainder of the Galaxy. Earth suffering impairment will gradually lose polar elasticity. This will cause the planet to ascend prematurely and in time, due to the sun's vicinity, shrivel in intense heat conditions with impaired hydrogen content and level. Man, if still inhabiting the earth would not survive in this intolerable climate of change.

Earth scorched by the intense heat of the sun, would become a giant fire ball finally disintegrating. This event marking the conclusion of the old phasing. After this a new earth will form out of a portion of the old, having similar marking and purposing. A new people will come to habitation, of higher spiritual intent and calibre. From their seed shall issue full Cosmic naturing which shall proclaim the natural law as invincible. Within their time, there shall be full chosen planetary ascension, unmarked by any premature conclusion or further destruction. Man and planet shall aspire together in joyful spiritual ascent.

Many souls returning from Earth will undergo a transitionary phase of "awaiting" until the requisite time for the birthing of the new Earth. They will be prepared for this initiation during Source sojourning and for the final phase which supports the later incarnation of those sufficiently evolved to protect the new Earth from that which led to former planetary extinction. The present Earth has been unable to achieve sustained patterns of growth, experiencing many necessary episodes of purification which have drawn destructive forces towards it. These resulting as part of the necessary purification process, which remains presently inconclusive. The future of the new planet militating towards a single focused point of evolutionary and spiritual growth will witness man and nature as moving together as one soul.

The final phase of Earth will be permanent and unmarked by Karmic penalty. It is perfected by the right action of man, who may assist it towards evolutionary completion.

30th April 1994

Your own solar system has zoned areas of intense gravitational pull which exercise a magnetic force field towards any planetary structure within that system showing pronounced instability. The vortex spiral existing between Mars and Jupiter attracts by powerful magnetism, weaker systems exhibiting defective orbiting. In the past, planets similar to your own entering this force field disintegrated. Particles still existing in space, presently assemble to meteorite action.

Earth presents similar propensities for disintegration should excessive weakening of its gravitational pull ensue.

This is a natural phasing taking place every so many billion years. Normally this phase of planetary change would not be due for many thousands of years. However unstable orbit if occurring prematurely, would create an accelerative process, thereby over-riding the natural cycle.

Man is creating an unstable climate where planetary uncertainty is forwarded in time. As we explained, this process, once activated, cannot be halted or voided if certain stages or trigger points are reached. This touching upon the point where your world stands gravely in risk of total decimation. Signals indicative of future world disintegration are not to be dismissed lightly. Those presently received by us indicate that there is a dangerous level of axial friction caused by an ongoing disturbance to earth, leading to severe earth tremor. This is being accelerated by man's experimental programmes above ground and below sea level. Shift triggered by earth vibration is caused by deep underground testing. This is giving rise to wide spread planetary shudder which we note to be well above normal and acceptable levels. At present we note an abnormal increase in volcanic activity coupled to sea level rise. We believe this is due to excessive earth movement and tremor.

We ask you to accept responsibility now for your Planet. It affords you life and well being during your sojourn here. You are dependant upon its continued stability. Man cannot at present exit to another sphere offering the same climatic suitability. Only one Earth may manifest at a time. Even with progress in space programming, man is not ready to infiltrate into other solar systems which would reject him environmentally. Artificial contrivances permitive of chemically induced adaptation to life within unsuitable and hostile planetary space will prove abortive.

You cannot envisage the holocaust which must eventually assemble. It will be irreversible, man subject to the most terrible scenario ever witnessed in the history of Earth. Gross forms of mutated life will be spawned, the result of genetic engineering. These mutants will arise as part man, part animal. The presence of animal implants within the human system, breaking natural laws will emerge in gross bestiality and hideous deformity of form.

This is the law of cause and effect. The soul in terrible shock will seek to leave the physical body. The remaining physical shell supporting only basic life, and at chemical level. Men will desire death in preference to the savagery of life upon earth as experienced in the aftermath of Doomsday. Only those sealed with the Light shall be afforded protection.

Thousands will meet death at the hands of their fellow man in the desperate battle for survival. Food shall be wrested from the mouth of the starving and eaten anew by those seeking vital sustenance. The dead will lie unburied upon the poisoned earth. Man may out of the sheer need for survival, eat the flesh of his own kind. Domestic animals who survive will not be afforded the luxury of food or shelter. Man will wrestle with them to eat the burnt grass of the field. Reverting to wild and demented states, rabid and diseased, and in desperate hunger, they will come from the hills in hordes to tear at the flesh of weakened man.

There will be no light from the sun. The wind carrying rife disease and pestilence to every land. In the darkness man will weep for the light of the morning, but it shall not be seen in his time again.

Children, return to the natural Law which protects, admit this law within your souls and the clear light of spirit. Petition that this time of destruction and sorrow may not come amongst you. Prevent it by the healing energy of love. Let it pass from your planet together with all Karmic penalties. We are at your side to encourage and to assist you. We presently stand in your midst with great love and concern.

Given to Earth in spiritual love 1st May 1994

Man's future residence will lie below the earth where he will exist in darkness. He will be unable to live at surface level, since heat will be at dangerously high levels. Children will not be born to man during this period since he will be infertile and women barren. This due to great radio activity leaking from nuclear stations which have been unsealed and stand open. Radiation will cause cancers in man contaminating vital airflow. Nuclear waste seeping into streams and rivers conducting to lethal doses in man and nature. Abnormal cross winds carrying dust particles of nuclear energy across the face of the earth.

It will be unsafe to drink water as this will see heavy contamination by diseases carried from masses of unburied bodies lying at surface level. Poisonous waste discharging from chemical industries and running into polluted rivers and streams will carry new breeds of bacteria for which there will be no antidote.

There will be years of famine, the earth ceasing to give man fruit in season. Nothing will grow upon earth until the time of the great purification is completed. Man sowing seed within darkened conditions, shall see this wither. Flesh falling away from his body, his bones will be seen, for he shall eat no more of the earths plenitude. Hand which once laboured shall be idle, he shall await glad release in death.

In those days the just will comfort and give succour to those who would otherwise despair. Their light penetrating to the deepest parts of the earth. They will traverse the planet in great spiritual safety and protection. Nothing shall harm them or come near to them. Their souls being fed with spiritual manna will be replenished. The physical body of these souls shall become transparent, their light seen illuminated within flesh.

They will come to Earth in great array taking up their abode until the day of great release when the natural law is satisfied. They will offer a service of unconditional love to those distressed souls remaining on earth, during the time of terrible upheaval. Particular soul groupings will discharge this main work during a phase where two thirds of the planet will suffer destruction. When they return to Source it will be without further desire or need to reincarnate again.

2nd May 1994

People living in the cities will experience greatest suffering. Life as they have known it will be irreversibly and permanently changed. Buildings disintegrating and falling will create total disruption everywhere. Exits from the cities and towns will be blocked with fallen masonry and debris. There will be no labour force to clear them. Man will run hither and thither in states of terror. The failure of essential services will disrupt supplies of water, electricity and gas rendering them obsolete. Whole cities will be cut off with communication at a standstill, whilst the machinery of modern technology will lie in ruins. There will be little vestige of a life style taken for granted by man only minutes before disaster struck with such terrible force and impact.

Food conservation and distribution will be severely affected, remaining supplies grossly contaminated by flood water and pollution. Debris giving rise to great clouds of dust impairing the respiratory system and making breathing critical. Main sewers will spew up contents by spasmodic ejection into streets and buildings, giving rise to wide spread cholera epidemics. New strains of resistant bacteria will swiftly a weakened immune system. Death will come to swiftly to many, to others slowly.

There will be disruption to every home and family. Parents and children, along with close kin witnessing enforced separation and death. They will be scattered and parted without any hope of reunion. Many families will evidence no surviving member. Many will leave the corpses of loved ones in sorrow and without the dignity of recognised burial. They will flee in great sorrow and tribulation and without possessions.

Strangers ministering to strangers, will elect new kin groups as an expediency measure, for protection and safety against great hordes of bestial and Godless men who shall descend upon them. In that day a life shall be forfeit for a shoe upon the foot, or clothes upon the body. Man exchanging these for an extension of his wretched existence. Many in that day will pray for death to release them. Man travelling forth seeking new shelter, will make his journey naked and unclothed, for in that day all men will possess nothing. They shall be as at the time of their birth. The physical body reflecting great sickness and disease will give expression to excessive grieving.

There will be many abortive attempts on the part of the unscrupulous to restore the status quo. Many false leaders emerging, will attempt to influence others by practising methods of vile profiteering. These men will barter the lives of others for gain. Their efforts will be abortive, for in the absence of technology which at one time balanced and distributed the earth's monetary systems, remaining currency will be valueless. There will be nothing man is able to buy or exchange with money! All that will concern him in that day is to examine the value of his own soul. Then he will petition ceaselessly for a further period of grace. For in Divine gracing is his ultimate Saviouring.

Sleep will come warily to man, for when he sleeps there is danger and risk to personal safety. Many will fear sleep not knowing if they will awaken. Many will long for its oblivion. Awakening serving only as a grim reminder and the knowledge that these events are irreversible. This will lead to periods of great retrospection, and ceaseless remorse. Many souls dying in despair and without future hope.

This is the given time of the Anti Christ, who will reign for a period, impressing great fear and terror into the hearts of men. Man's spirit shall fail him as he looks upon the savage deeds of unspiritual leaders. Only the light of his soul shall saviour him, setting his feet upon the sure hill of salvation. He shall come to witness time as a mirage and illusion. There will spring up a new desire to enter into immortality and by the power of the spirit. Then all worlds and kingdoms processing before him shall show swift passing and fleeting glory.

His feet shall stand upon the new earth. He shall come into the kingdom of spiritual peace and light.

3rd May 1994

After the time of great tribulation there shall be a new peace. Man resting within his spiritual nature will in loving trust restore and heal the ravaged Earth. Many years may elapse before this witnesses completion, for man must endure and experience that which he has engendered by his own accountable action.

During the time of great purification, there will be a deliberate turning towards higher thought and an increase in spiritual motivation. Surviving man shall come to recognise the traumatic events of the planetary holocaust and its subsequent aftermath, as a held in energy, which when dispersed, moves towards the day of great release setting into action the reverse side, which is spiritual wholeness and balance.

Man and Nature are ever one. When nature moves out of balance and stability, man suffers the inevitable penalty. There is however, a relevant turning point leading to the overall oneing of both in a new and purposeful partnership, recreating paradise upon earth. When this is reached, there is movement towards new spiritual growth.

Even now there is hope that the grim events set out in the prophecies may be alleviated. These will be moderated in the case of souls who have not incurred or merited such severe Karmic penalties. The natural law will be satisfied here. These souls developing an immunity protective of the nervous system will escape the full experience attached to harsh and bitter survival. Nevertheless, they will witness the world and peoples in their hour of agony, weeping for late salvation and deliverance. Their tears alone shall moisture the arid ground restoring the spirit to despairing man. Within this grouping of souls many have awaited reincarnation until this final phase. They are aware of their accountability and will discharge loving service with great spiritual intent and responsible purposing.

All will witness to the manifestation of Angelic beings who until that moment, have remained hidden amongst men. They already stand in your world. Awakened souls are perceiving their presence. Many souls will see them long before the holocaust as man accustoms to high Cosmic energies which link men to their spiritual self. They shall be seen as a great array of translucent rainbowed light, greater than the numbers of stars and the grains of sand upon the sea shore. Arising, with lazers of Cosmic lightning in their hands they shall wage war against the anti Christ and his kingdom. When he and his followers are finally displaced and victory won, they shall touch the great wounds of earth in loving benediction, and with powerful healing restore earth and man to former beauty and glory. Then the soul shall ascend, carried upon their great wings to spiritual inheritance, and immortal Source indwelling.

Earth shall be healed, restored to pristine beauty and light, symbolically integrated within the Universal whole. There shall be no further destruction of her person, nor shall she perish, held within the Cosmic web of timelessness. In that day there shall be joyful reunion and gathering of the soul elect who rejoice in her peacefulness and light.

4th May 1994

You must understand that there is no fearful vengeance due to men from the accumulation of past, present even future misdeeds. God who is pure light sits not in personal judgement upon you. It is rather the rebalancing and re-alignment of broken natural laws which stand in need of correction. Man has constantly abused these without remorse or conscience. Universal laws affect and govern all issued matter. They are laws of cause and effect. Broken, they affect overall balance and ongoing stability.

Man is destroying the essential qualities of an earth who is the great Mother and natural provider of life. A wounded and dying planet depleted in life force is emerging directly as the result of his uncaring attitude. The future legacy of such action carries implicit and bitter penalties for Earth and man.

There is growing evidence of increased planetary instability. This may be corrected if man assumes right responsibility by exercising proper guardianship towards the earth he inhabits. Failure in this direction moves him closer to uncertain events, disastrous in nature, these events will render him subject to the unleashed force of nature. There can be no compromise at that stage. It will be too late to look or search for curative measures. This is the final phasing.

Light and love counterbalance negativity. Every single loving thought elevates energy levels by creating positive light waves heal and correct planetary imbalance. We still witness insufficient input in this direction. Light centres should be set up by souls in groups who by amplifying love energy, send it out powerfully to a stricken world. As this energy is released, man becomes powerfully drawn towards light and spiritual purpose, which in turn creates a positive environment. The overall and accumulative effect of love can transform the world, healing everything within its radius.

The first sign signifying future world disasters will be that of increasing fear and apprehension growing to storm force within the hearts of men. This disquiet coupled to inward conflict will create a spirit of great restlessness. This is the seed of the Anti Christ seeking to infiltrate every heart, by chaos and confusion.

The second portent will be evidence of growing corruption in leaders whose sole commitment is to warring conquests. This energy matches to the assembling form of evil and destructive intent. War for the sake of war will be engineered by godless men, who harness its robotic force for personal advantage and gain. This energy will spread, breathed in by many souls. It will be recognised by a dull metallic taste in the mouth, having an undefinable repellent smell. Its odour when absorbed into the physical body will be the cause of gross disorder and great sickness of soul.

The third sign will be advancement in genetic engineering, creating a future grotesque and lethal species. These mutants will be marked with the sign of the Anti Christ, dominating the world for a considerable time. Their fruits will be excessively bitter for those who taste them, they will immerse many souls in dark despair. Seeking the destruction of light, they will carry banners of great darkness into every corner of the world. powerfully overwhelming, and captivating many souls to bondage.

The fourth sign will be eventual collapse of existing planetary structure and composition. The life force of earth in slow decline will exhibit grossly abnormal climatic conditions. Accererated temperature change will be intolerable. Slowed orbital spin creating massive geographical upheaval. Earth will orbit closer to its sun incurring excessive heat even in the most moderate climes. Harmful ultra violet ray absorption will access to man, causing gaping and cancerous holes throughout his body. There will be no protection from this radiation, except the given immunity of the light body.

Rapid heat rise will spawn many mutant species, these emerging from the deep core of the earth and surfacing, will display predatory and dangerous natures. These reptiles will inhabit earth as long as the evil of the Anti Christ exists, and are the outward manifestation of that vile energy. Life force at its weakest, will slow man to inert and sluggish nature. He will perform at the level of a beast, until such time as his purification complies with and satisfies the natural law. Final completion will witness to his spiritual re-seating and elevation to original divine naturing.

All those who have subscribed to the Anti Christ will be confined to the lowest dimensions in the bowels of the Earth, being bound in fetters to that allegiance they have followed. They shall be eventually freed by the loving petitions of the soul elect, who weep for their plight and work ceaselessly for their re-admittance to light. This phasing following upon sure deliverance of the Earth from that energy and sign. All then will be sealed to eternal grace and saving. Amen, Amen, Praise and endless Adoration always to the Divine Nature of the Source whose inbreathing all men shall become.

5th May 1994

PREFACE TO CHANNELLED VISIONING.

Visioned channelling integrates the psychic faculty met fully within the spiritual. Here the use of creative visualization is linked to states of altered consciousness which are keyed into the subconscious mind, signalled at conscious level and interpreted by learnt and acquired literacy.

Primary channelling comes from given information which commands less by way of visual content. It is signalled by the higher self, opening the spiritual mind to full ability by pooling into the collective unconscious. It is the main container for esoteric knowledge and accessed at higher entry points lying outside normal consciousness. This type of channelled message is generally given through the transmitted thought of higher energies who provide significant guidance and chosen material throughout.

Secondary channelling is mainly pictorial, transmitted through the powerful visual imagery of the psyche which is activated to draw material, significant in content, depicting symbolic meaning. This forms a powerful link with the subconscious mind, affecting and charging stronger energy input. Pictures often archetypal are depicted in strong primitive colouring and line which invite appropriate frequencies and elevated mind responses.

Tertiary channelling is of the pure visioning kind, where the channeller having fully contacted the higher self is able to draw from that self spontaneously by merely "tuning in," There is always detachment in an experience where the channeller becomes an essential part of the process. By witnessing to the involvement of the self within creative visualization, there is a powerful ability to retain incoming information, enabling the brain to witness an event, by writing about it simultaneously and with great accuracy throughout its actual experiencing.

This process may be compared to lucid dreaming during which the channeller is conscious of events at one level and experiences them in altered states at another. The two states overlap without noticeable discomfort or disorientation. The end result is a balanced combination of prophecy and divination contained within given syntax. The following channelled visioning follows this tertiary pattern.

May 1994

I saw the whole earth winnowed, whilst the straw and worthless chaff was blown to the four winds whose faces are ever turned towards the face of the Cosmos. In that moment all was gathered into the breath of the Universal good and being plenteously stored was regiven to earth in goodly and generous measure. I saw the mouthing of the soil opened and thirsty, receiving the goodliness of the four elements who dispensed in solicitude that required to bring to harvesting and fertile fruiting. Then the land was quiet and prayer filled with great benediction and blessing.

I saw the inhabitants of the land lauding and praising the Great good who had given all things into their hands for sake keeping. I witnessed their hearts opening and large with the great crimson thoughts of loving. I beheld their purity rising like a wave of clear water laving all within its radius to sweet cradling.

Then the sound of their praise echoed in my ears like a thousand bees, droning in honeyed flowers. In my joining I rose up like a fountain of clear crystal tunement whose melody lay beyond all known music and scented anthems. Upon this note I entered into the realms of light, standing within the spun rainbows of The Cosmos. I became the Cosmos in oneness, held timelessly in seconds of blissfulness.

I looked down upon my physical body, scanning its inertness and having measure of its pain and heaviness. I floated above it, in the amazing lightness of new form merging with the headiness of pure unbreathed air. In that moment I opened to a true dimension of self which is presently unadmitted and withheld from the eye of man. As I touched upon the fabric of my soul, I was immediately immersed within its unsullied richness and divine naturing. With infinite gazing, I beheld all things, past present and future meeting within the single eye of vision. This transformation forming into a rainbowed bridge of light which spanned Earth and met heaven at the point of intermeshing frequencies

In growing stature, I saw all nature as one force forming within me in ascending harmony and full understanding. The powerfulness of the eagle entered into me as I soared upwards and into the light of the sun. Safely vantaged at last and held securely by the great pinions of Grace, I dared to breathe, the very name of self. In that moment healing was given, and wholeness restored.

7th May 1994

Taken above the perimeter of the Universe, I looked down upon the Earth below. In the semblance of a small seed, I saw myself growing into the form of a great tree. This displaying greenness and leaf, afforded shade to those sheltering beneath its branches, protecting them from the heat of the noonday sun. The branches opening out from the girth of the trunk grew tall embracing the sky, showering fragrant scented blossom which emerging from the hiatus of new budding fulfilled the promised season of spring.

The fullness of summer exciting sap to increased flow, showed rapid growth within a vast antennae of extending branches. Birds of the air dwelling in the tree and joined to its energy, nested and slept.

Swarming insect life attracted towards the budding flowers hastened fertilization, activating these towards ultimate fruiting. Eventual ripening showering fruit and yielding an abundance of realized maturity. Throughout many cycles, and with roots lying deeply submerged beneath ground level, the tree would seek deeper moisture enabling it to drink more freely from earth's admixture which nurtured it even in seasons of excessive dryness and heat.

In seasons of wintering, the tree prior to resting, would release a thousand golden leaves to fall earthwards, covering sleeping earth with a blanket layer of warmth. As the winter was levered, the leaves finally disintegrating became one with soil composition, utilized for future seasonal growth, nutrition and cycle. Nature returns whatever is taken from earth in repetitive cycle.

I saw with insight, that the life cycle of the tree closely symbolized inner growth and spiritual flowering. The life of the soul lies hidden within spiritual energy. It buds, flowers and fruits within given season by the action of imparted grace. Nurtured by spiritual energy, it puts forth new growth in loving expectation. The soul, similar to the tree aspires upwards moving towards spiritual maturity.

The rings denoting the life of the tree and seen when cut open, match to the incarnatory cycles of the soul. The soul also has many life cycles during which growth takes place, and where fruiting and seeding follows in seasonal climate. Fed with spiritual sustenance it is also replenished by vital life force, at hidden level. The tree growing above the ground and moving towards the sky, shows the deep desire of every soul to ascend, finally returning to Source. Although its roots lie deeply below the earth's surface, it still a living thing even when there is no outward sign of visible life. This phase indicating that life even within the deep sleep of winter is temporary having new cycles of awakening which promote new growth within due season. I witnessed my soul sleeping within awaiting its hour of awakening. The warm light of the spiritual sun giving it joyful expression, clothed it in glorious apparel.

9th May 1994

I saw a huge net containing all manner of living things being taken up into safety. The net remained unbroken although many wild beasts clawed at it as it was lifted far above the earth, attempting to savage and defile it. It was sealed with the mark of that Guardian whose duty it was to bring it intact into the realms of safe keeping for as long as the Great Beast reigned.

I saw that life within the net was marked with a Divine seal of protection and that it was unbroken during the time of passage. The light which encompassed the net was full of eyes which kept continuous watchful vigilance and great prayerfulness. The creatures within the net slept soundly being unmindful of the great perils which surrounded them as they were swung upwards and away from the Earth's minding. They were unlike any earth forms I had seen, being covered entirely in brilliant diamond facets which shone like jewelled stars. Upon their heads were the triple crowns of future kingdoms which were to come latterly into great Wisdom and Truth. The net rested upon the four elements being surely carried by them into the great breath of the Immortal Spirit.

Many came to covet the privilege accorded them in honour due. All covering their eyes against bright light emanating from their pure spirits. These were of translucent appearance, their life structure observable, thinly veiled through the covering of flesh. All men paid homage and rendered praise as they were seen to ascend.

I was given to understand that these were the manifested soul elect who had earned by virtue of loving service shown to humanity, immunity against the incurred penalties of Karmic signing. Upon them is conferred a crown of light which shall be placed over the single eye, symbolic of Divine Source indwelling. They are removed for a period from Earth, existing within higher dimensional entry.

When they are returned in full glory and might, all shall kneel before them in reverence and fear. Their eye, fired by the pure vision of the Cosmos shall be terrible to behold, men shall turn away from their powerful light. Then the darkness of the enemy will be vanquished and all shall come into the Great Peace.

10th May 1994

As I looked towards the earth, I saw the face of the planet assume a different shape. Drawing in its final breath, and in great distress and pain, it compressed all nature and man as one, impressing upon the surface great flatness and eveness of distribution. Every particle of matter in this showing became inert, lifeless and shrivelled. This signifying the great emptying of man and the ultimate withdrawal of that energy bestowed upon him as life force. In that moment there was universal death.

Then I saw all matter arise, healed and filled with a new breathing. As man arose he spewed out out his mouth the remnant of that which was contrary to spiritual action. This necessary to the intake of new breath which when inhaled, drew purposeful intent and bestowed wholeness.

The shape of this spiritual energy was rounded and full, entering both earth and men and restoring former depletion. Then man stood up with the stature of a giant, whilst out of his mouth issued the pure flame of spirit. This manifested as a white symbol having eight equal parts and angles, representative of octagonal shaping and of rainbowed hue. To all but the spiritual, this sign remained hidden from sight. All things being covered with its flame were renewed to Source light. All manner of gifts were given to him who received its benisons, whilst Earth rose up to greet a new Saviouring. Nature pouring out an abundance of life upon him, enfolded him into her great heart. Gaia saluting him as a true son and heir.

All tribulation ceased and men walking upon the Earth were clothed in new truth and wisdom. I saw their understanding powerfully joined to the Source greatly inclined towards spiritual purpose and intention. I heard the sound of their great wings as they, together with the Earth ascended to those heavenly dimensions which await the spirit.

11th May 1994

Looking upwards towards the sky, I saw the formation of a small cloud which gathered other clouds as it moved nearer to the Earth. As it increased in size and volume, I saw that it was of transparent colour, showing a speckled consistency. The cloud hovering above the earth and coming into contact with the atmosphere, quickly released moisture. Large drops fell to the ground assuming the shape of miniature suns. The particles when mixing with water and air, emitted a sweet cloying smell, pungent, yet not at unacceptable level. As it touched the ground, these spherical drops multiplied, upon bursting disclosing a densely packed yellow substance which quickly spreading at ground level, influenced the normal growth cycle of all coming into contact with it.

Everything, including earth and sky became coloured and saturated with this strange substance. On contact the molecular structure of existing life forms were radically altered by its energy. Many gigantic formations of leaf and flower sprang up showing mutational change, disclosing gross distortion and aberration.

Where rapid structural change occurred, the ground was seen to open, displaying the stratum of previous civilizations embedded in igneous volcanic action. When the mass of long submerged land reappeared, there was seen the spirit of the age itself, manifesting in complete or incomplete phasing. Men of that time arose from that which was non existent, extolling present man to repair that which he had laid waste.

Then the souls of men were stirred to great spiritual deeds, distressed and confounded as they became by the significance of these events. When they stood together as one in the light places, all was seen as an illusion and mirage. Then there was restoration to proper marking in time and space. The noxious substance which had infected all earth and form finally dispersed. When other clouds returned, there was an abundant pouring of natural moisture which ultimately replenished and healed the Earth, restoring all matter to ordered sequence. Then men of spirit witnessed the destruction of evil which was removed for ever from the earth.

12th May 1994

I saw a transparent prism hung over the earth distributing white light as rainbowed colour, this covered all men. The energy of the prism was magnetic, drawing all towards it's powerful rays. At its highest point the triangular composition attracted the light of the Cosmos, whilst at it's base it accumulated the condescension of emitted Source energy. This was poured out upon the earth with great accuracy. The process consisted of entered and held electro magnetic beams discharged within a spiralling vortex and encircling that which contained the phial of purification.

I saw two Angels descend from heaven holding the prism within their hands. Their faces were turned towards the light of the sun reflecting a spectrum of colour inundating all within the rainbowed circle. They constantly turned the prism so that it faced to every part of the earth. As it was turned, all men came into its light and were transfigured. It was given to some men to enter directly into the prism and to become part of its configuration. They ascended within its sealing to Source level, being impressed with the indelible mark of Divine showing

For a time they remained within galaxies, light years away, and at higher dimensional level. There they were granted understanding and wisdom unrelated to any previous knowledge or learning of man. They became futured to the time when matter showed only in the spiritual counterpart, and were as pure energy, manifesting as bright suns. They themselves transformed by prismatic light, re-entered the earth in this signalling, awakening the hearts of many.

In this showing I saw many prisms containing souls of pure beings who had elected to Saviour the earth at a time of great and dire need. I saw the prisms open to disclose angelic beings who had remained for many ages within the vicinity and protection of Source light. These now descended to Earth to succour men and to revive many who had it not been for their assistance, would have perished. Their love was visibly seen by the sign of the great heart of the Cosmos, which rested and pulsated upon their brow. By this sign they were joined to that boundless energy from which they drew in endless and continuous stream. This was offered to mankind who were birthed into new life and spiritual signing. Then praise was in the mouth of all men who dwelt within this light.

13th May 1994

I was carried by the great winds of the Cosmos to witness the spiritual rebirthing of man. As I travelled towards the Cosmic Sun, I was caught up in a mighty tide of amber coloured nuclei. As this moved towards me in myriad form, I was swept along with it. As it came nearer, I saw it greatly magnified in composition. Looking closely at what appeared to be millions of single amber coloured, transparent cells or chambers I saw many sleeping souls. They were closely emmeshed within an amber liquid and although securely held, floated therein. Myriad unborn souls lay in foetal stages of development, embryonically positioned.

111

Looking again, I saw them growing to great size and structure, emerging through the single chamber into which they had been seeded. Then they descended to earth taking up their abode within flesh. Here they were exiled and in great pain, petitioning for Source sight which was withdrawn from them for a time.

I came to look upon them for the third time and saw them ascend within other chambers admitting them in full maturity. These chambers resembled the physical structure of the human heart having similar composition. The hearts were linked to Central Source energy which nurtured and fed them during their returning journey with much loving and advantaging. Then there was an assembling and joining of all souls. As they ascended, they merged into one journeying, each having a silver filigree or line which attached them securely to the Great Web of Source inbreathing. The length of the silver line was shortened as they were taken into the Great Heart of the Universal breath.

My ears echoed with the sound of praise they rendered to That Energy which had rebirthed them to joyful re-admittance of Source Light. I saw them enter into the mouth of the Source as a flowing fire of whitened flame. As I looked again, I saw them descend and ascend in countless repetitive action. Then I understood that this process of birth and rebirth was a never ending cycle, and one whose Divine movement was the ceaseless action of Grace. I saw the mighty spirit of the Uncreate enter and re-enter man in countless incarnatory cycle. Then I understood that final and ultimate re-entry lay within spiritual completion.

14th May 1994

Angelic beings always retain sight of Source indwelling, and are unable by virtue of their heavenly origins to withhold praise. Ceaseless homage and adoration form an integral part of their nature. They have no experience of fallen naturing. Man by reason of his fall from grace inhabits an emotional and physical body which is joined to the spiritual. He alone is graced with free choice to offer or withhold praise, and it is in that spirit of joyful choice he becomes rightly attuned to Divine insightfulness and awareness.

Praise amplifies love energy which ascending beautifies and amplifies the Universal Good. It is never effaced since it is retained at the highest level, becoming integrated and woven within the pure vibration of Source inbreathing.

I saw the praise of man ascend to enter into the mouth of the Source becoming greatly enhanced and causing great joy therein.

17th May 1994

I saw the hand of God reach out to touch the spirit of man. In that infinite moment he was uplifted in grace beholding the face of His Creator. Cradled in the vortex of time, all worlds and galaxies birthed and dissolved before him in an endless moment of infinite gazing. He came to witness the action of bright stars, birthed within timelessness. All substance he then touched appearing as a mirage, lay outside reality. Only he was real, only he existed, only God was presently before him. Everything else was as an illusion. The communion between his soul and the Uncreate in that moment, fusing as one eternal thought.

In that single moment he entered into the total understanding and concept of Creative Thought, and was held within the Great Heart of the Source. In that holding there was no movement, nothing existed except the womb of great silencing and peace.

In stillness he was one with that Divine energy which enfolded him, nor would he chose otherwise, since in that holding, all was wrapped in unsurpassing sweetness and light. Within that mighty silence, he was admitted to the resonance of every living thing which had continued expression within a single note into which he joyfully merged. Ascending into the essence and energy of the Cosmic note, he was naught except within spiritual knowing.

I witnessed man beholding his soul, seeing him weep for sheer wonder at its beauty and pure form. It appeared as a perfect imprintation, and in the image of the Source, so that when he looked towards it, and from every angle, he saw reflected his own spiritual nature which was ever inseparably linked to that Love which had originally created him. This appeared to sustain and prolong that final moment of Creative Loving which would eventually reach him to certain immortality.

18th May 1994

All appeared before me in great clarity and light. I heard the voice of the Great Uncreate breaking as thunderous sound, darting like lightning into the souls of men. His body manifesting, shone like burnished gold. Between the gold there appeared delicate interwoven strands which contained myriad souls held and nurtured by crimson flowing streams of love which extending from his open heart. The heart composed of delicate fibres and extending upwards towards His brow, burned fiercely showing as red hot coals. The fire consuming all within its heat, purified those who entered it's unquenchable flame.

As these souls emerged from the fire, they were seen to be wrapped around in a wondrous light, the seeing of which surpassed all visioning. They by absorption and by close inhalation of Cosmic breathing, had assumed the singular properties peculiar to that Divine energy. The inheritance of Cosmic light bestowed upon them a visible sign of Source indwelling and grace.

As they emerged, all stood within great fountains of spiralling light, revealing every part of the physical body, showing to the minutest capillary. This manifested the ongoing flow of moleculed composition and energy, outlined in great clarity and amazing detail. The elevation of flesh showed the inlining and compassionate nature of the Godhead Who had condescended to take up His abode within man, and with such overwhelming love that it was miraculous to behold; giving great humbling and thanks. The spiritual and physical now merged together, joining as one within the cloaking of the Light Body, each composite part showing the other to full meriting and glory. I was given to understand that this is the only body of ascension.

There is no part of man separate or unjoined in God, there is no part of God which is not truly met and realized within man. All form one corporate body of light which continually irradiates the Universe. The true composition of ascending Cosmic essence and energy is the God-man.

20th May 1994

I saw the Christus shedding great tears for the sins of men. He stood in every age with outstretched arms, bidding souls to come to Him. Each of His tears were gathered by angels to assuage those who were admitted to his light and truth. I saw many silver chalices containing these tears. Angels conveying the chalices to a great height, lovingly poured out their precious contents upon the face of the earth in healing.

I saw the great hands of the Christus move in loving benediction to bless and cover the earth. From His hands, great wounds appeared, shining like jewels, I saw these wounds open, pouring their crimson tide over men.

All receiving His blood were filled with a new spirit, and became as other Christs, succouring a multitude of souls. I saw hosts of angels descending to earth at His bidding. Each bore the imprint and seal of Source indwelling. Many standing within the radius of this angelic light, became empowered to teach by spreading the word of the Christus. These souls grew to great beauty and radiance illuminating many places, and setting free those who were held in great spiritual captivity.

I saw the new Christus descend to earth, wearing a crown of rainbowed light upon His head in which were positioned many eyes which appeared to open in symbolic sequence and sightfulness. Every eye was focused upon the single Eye of the Source, this alone carried the vision of immortal life, which was given to all men. Then the eyes within the crown of the Christus became as bright stars falling down from Cosmic ordering, and touching man with powerful insight. As man's sightfulness opened fully, he was given to see through a mystical eye, which accorded rightful visioning. All then was purposed to perfect ordering and full Cosmic gazing.

Many ascended masters were seen, conversing with the Christus, whilst angels held the great train which contained all souls admitted to His light. The earth shook with their resonant vibration which preceded the new birthing of Spirit. Then men opened their mouths to prophecy, this gift emerging in the form of a great wind which sweeping across the Universe, entered filling the hearts of many. Men shook with the powerful force of this wind, when it departed they were seen to be purified and filled with the undulating waves of Cosmic light which reached them to the shores of Paradise.

20th May 1994

In a dream I was given a timepiece to hold. The timepiece was of circular shaping of great circumference and dimension. Suspended upon a huge leather strap, which showed much wear, it was heavy and cumbersome. I saw the impossibility of wearing it with any degree of ease or comfort.

The casing of the watch appeared to be made of a curious and unknown metallic substance. As I looked I saw it open into three parts which disclosed intricate workings. The first part showed the beginning of time, and as I looked upon the huge wheels and cogs which appeared to be fashioned out of a dullish silver, I was amazed by their complex intricacy and workmanship. These parts grew larger in size, eventually reaching gigantic proportions. I was shown the third part of the watch which I understood portrayed the end of time. This was cast in the same silver substance as the first, having similar moving parts and showing amazing accuracy.

I saw the central portion of the watch open, disclosing the cycles of man from his origins to his final closing. Many of the pictures turning as pages in an illustrated book, were depicted in strong primitive colouring. When the watch was closed the three parts were seen simultaneously through a kind of transparent fabric which disclosing all compartments came to be viewed within the perfected action of synchronized and faultless timing.

I clearly remembered the watch with its intricate detail and strange compartmentalization on awakening, finding I still held the imprinted image at conscious level. Asking for the significance of this lucid dreaming, I was given the following information.

The watch is the self, its compartments matching to universal cycles of birth, life and death. The three fold configuration a reminder that man is required to complete all evolutionary cycles in the time afforded him within each incarnation.

The passing of time stands symbolically for mans capacity towards spiritual growth. This from seed to full maturity and fruiting within given sight of harvesting.

I understood that the time clock could be not be set to another period outside present dimensional experiencing, although there was resetting to commencement altered timing within each stepped and realized dimensional entry. The clock remaining closed during each incarnatory cycle was to be opened only at the end of each completed phase. Then it would spontaneously show all three compartments, affording man an opportunity to witness and examine spiritual growth within particular and allotted time sequences.

The ascension of man was seen held and contained within a great shout of praise in which I saw him uplifted to the Source. His praisefulness appeared like a great showering of golden particles which were purposefully elevated towards that dimension which admitted them worthily. Every one of the particles was composed of great light and of enhanced vibrational composition. This structuring, emulating the resonance and openness of Cosmic sounding.

As this energy ascended, it was amplified by a clear pool of residual praise which when meted out in equal parts, served to conduct man to full spiritual orchestration. Then sound fusing echoed that particular vibration which opening the gates of heaven admitted all to full glorying.

Then I saw life and form bow low, merging to enter into tranfused ascension, which was contained within rainbowed light and great loving. This ascending energy releasing its sweet essence formed into a second note. When this note was amplified it tranformed all within its resonance into one single action of spiritual gracing.

I saw this gathered together and spiral upwards, emerging as myriad star points of golden light which found integration within a single point. Fusing as one energy, it entered into the mouth of the Source Itself, where it finally merged with Divine inbreathing. Here it sounded praise in endless vibrational note, it's resonance held timelessly by the Logos or Word of God, which is the Uncreate.

I saw the great note of mans praise recreated endlessly and made acceptable to the opened Heart of the Creative thought which embracing it, enhanced all men to further gracing.

25th May 1994

In this visioning I witnessed to the amazing love poured out upon man.

I saw the compassion of the Source who is unable to withhold love even for the duration of one second. I was drawn rapidly towards the open mouth of the Godhead, remaining cradled within His breath. In that moment of timelessness, there was the blissfulness of being held within that loving, of resting within powerful sweetness which saturated my entire being. I knew that in this single moment, all I could ever experience within the past, present or future, was shown as now. I spun within the splendour of enhanced dimensions, entering into the Infinite which conveyed the silence and the peace of the Great Uncreated Thought.

I saw a great outpouring of love manifesting as bright colours releasing flowing streams of Cosmic light. These manifesting as stars of great luminosity, outshone the most brilliant jewel. As they moved towards the Earth's atmosphere, they darted into the opened hearts of mankind. I could see their light glowing within and shining transparently. By many radiations of love, they entered all souls with great fragrancing.

This contagious love spread widely throughout the Universe until all were embued by its transfusive energy. Then I saw each heart open wide to attract that Divine Loving in which man ascends by joining to that spiritual counterpart within. This taking place in great healing and wholeness.

In that moment there was joy and glad visioning as man beheld the purpose of spiritual intent which drew him powerfully towards the Source. In that transition there was an understanding of the deliberateness of a Love which recalled him so strongly. I saw him arise as from a deep sleep, standing in the light of his own empowerment, and with great dignity, before the threshold of the Source.

Then all men came into much light and glory, colour and sound merging expressed the purest synchronicity and melody within a great Amen. Men became filled with rapture and ecstacy causing them to leave their physical bodies, ascending in light to the gate of heaven. The sweetness of the Cosmic note calling them, so that they ascended in their purest form. Then their souls merged into the patterned frequency of spirit.

As the earth body dropped away from them, I saw them enter into a great body of light, becoming finally absorbed into the Source Itself. After this I saw them no more, for in this dimension they had become as pure energy, without form or physical sighting. They were as refined air which bestowed upon them, Divine inbreathing.

26th May 1994

As I looked towards the sun, I saw an eagle and a dove flying far above the earth. Each carried the seed of the Logos. They flew at the same height, and within the same flight pathway. As both came closer to each other they met. Upon touching, one appeared to merge into the composition of the other finally melding and taking new shape. This integration showing a combination of the unique qualities of both, I saw there was no separation.

The opposite strengths of powerfulness and sweetness combining, produced the fused qualities of spiritually enhanced purity. There was no dominant quality overshadowing the other. The fierce qualities of the Eagle were perfectly balanced and complemented by the sweetness and gentleness of the Dove.

This overlapping occurs within the spiritual level when man comes into direct lining with that which purposes him to the Source. Divine fusing is composed of those opposite energies which combining powerfully, furnish the fertile ground of spiritual intent. Only then is man completely fulfilled. Then he soars upwards as an Eagle with great clarity and vision realizing the highest expression of self. As the Dove, he seeks with purity and strength that inner peace which is expressive of great loving.

Both Eagle and Dove are winged, symbolizing man's ceaseless desire for ascension and his ultimate release from earth binding. Although his feet rest firmly upon the earth which birthed him, his higher self dreams always of flight. Both elements of earth and air represent aspects of soul freedom in which the spiritual attracts the physical to ascend to Source Light. It is only within completed balance and integration of both higher and lower selves that man may attain to a spiritually perfected state.

I saw again the Eagle and the Dove. This time I did not see them integrate, each went separate ways, flying in opposite directions and conserving their unique qualities. I saw in this, the fragmentation and separation of body and soul within physical and the spiritual. Division within the higher and lower self leads to isolation from each complementary part. Then there is failure to seed requisite qualities which bring man into spiritual peace and wholeness.

30th May 1994

I saw the word PRAISE emitting from the mouth of the Source, making loud and thunderous sound which echoed throughout heaven. I saw the word form into a triumphal arc of light as it entered into every dimension before reaching Earth. There it paused before reaching the souls of men who trembled in admittance of its resonance. As I looked, I beheld a merging of note creating a cascading flow of music, which melted the hearts of men to glad weeping. Then every mouth was opened to the great glorification of He who Is as all worshipped and ascended.

Taken up into the Holy Mount, I saw the purity of light emanating from the Source caused men to avert their gaze. When they looked upwards their earth forms dissolved as the spirit broke through the bounds of common flesh. They were seen to be transfigured and irradiated, entering into the union of light. Then I heard the song of many angels mingling with the praise of men as all were joined in rapturous adoration

The vibration of that sound moved heaven and earth. I saw them lifted up and disappearing from sight. Then there appeared to be neither Heaven or Earth for both had ascended, elevated and taken up into the third kingdom of spirit which lies above all, and is the seat of pure Source light and blissfulness. In that moment there was no created thing except a great void of light which was presently to birth.

I became part of that Void and Cosmic birthing. I saw myself as a tiny speck of energy let into being. Then accelerating faster than the speed of light assembling to matter and form. My ears resounding with the mighty rhythm and resonance of praise reached me into many creatured wombs in time and timelessness.

I am that praise, for it is the self who refashions in pure ascendancy of note that joyful experience and breathing. Every pulse and heart beat echoes its vibrancy. I hear it within the silence of unuttered thought. When the soul is slipped from the body in sleep, I enter into its endless song. Within states of consciousness I flow in that love tide.

30th May 1994

I saw all things beholden unto His eye which encompassed in great love and compassion; Creation. This divine action of single gazing held in powerful focus and screening every form of life which came before it. I saw the great openness of this eye, knowing that there was no closing to sleep, and that every moment of Source gazing was filled with great compassion and loving. The eye revolving in constant circular motion, brought all created matter into its field of vision simultaneously.

In the midst of the eye was a brilliant sun emitting golden shafts of light. These rays penetrating the Earth, saturated man and nature to great desire and longing. I saw the light of this sun dancing with rainbowed colour, touching the heart where it kindled a spiritual spark of soul light, opening the spirit to great and wondrous enjoinment. I saw man elevated, breathless with praise and adoration, silent in wordless wondering.

I understood that this gracing was the moment and the giving of a soul to man, realizing that he could never aspire to anything higher than that bestowed upon him in such sweetness and compassion. The single eye of the Source was to be visioned before the soul at all time, and in every place, even darkened. This standing as the token sign of sought sonship and Divine parenting. Man searching for this spiritual gift would ultimately prize it above all other consideration and temporal possession.

I saw the eye of the Source searching for those souls who stood yet within His gazing, although without spiritual insightfulness. These were signalled to angelic beings whose composition was allied to that of His substance. They carried and brought these souls into sighted alignment with great enhancement and gracing. The Source seeing every soul as His creation and therefore good, absorbed all matter resting within Its Infinite gazing. As the all seeing Eye beheld time and timelessness as one Universal second, It counted all men to paradise.

Then the Eye of the Source, shed and let fall a single tear which was composed of pure white and glistening light. The tear separated to form into many eyes which I saw to be exact replicas of the original, although smaller. These birthing to angelic form were positioned above the Great Single Eye, keeping ceaseless vigilance and watchfulness over all created worlds and galaxies. In the midst of these guardians, I witnessed the imprinting of the Source which shining as pure gold signified the unbroken covenant of the Uncreate.

6th June 1994

I saw a great array of angelic beings carrying with them coloured bands of energy which illuminated Earth by restoring it to former spiritual empowerment. These arcs of energy irradiating everything within their pathway left all imbued with sweet and resonating love, moving men to open their hearts, thereby admitting pulsating waves of healing light which renewed and greatly purified. As this process took place, there was an immediate lowering and divesting of the Ego, permitting man to enter into new spiritual formation and dimension. Then the higher self magnified flesh to divine spontaneity and spiritual birthing.

I saw many angels arising in mighty formation surrounding these souls and expressing great rapture. They had witnessed a miracle, never before evidenced. Man in his finest flowering hour exceeding the angelic host in expression and the dignity of spiritual freedom.

This act of metamorphosis witnessed the earth bound creature, exalted, elevated and transfigured by Divine energy, exuding powerful Cosmic charging. Then the earth body of man was glorified, emerging from past chaining of the conditioned self.

I saw men and angels uniting together in jubilant rejoicing and untiring psalmody. As their forms merged, they became as one soul intertwined by the spiritual bonds of love and devotion. I saw them rise higher and higher until they were seen no longer having entered into the threshold of the Source. Their sound as they ascended appeared at first as a low murmuring. As I listened I heard this sound grow into a mighty rushing crescendo which held the unsung melody of Creation. Then there was nothing except a mighty silence filling the heart to overflowing, manifesting as spectrumed light rainbowing fast into the Universal heart where it was eternally held.

I saw the Oneness of all things having similarity to the repetitive action of a single breath, and emitting Universal energy. This pulsating energy was re-gathered and absorbed by a cycled vortex action of the indrawn breath. I saw this breath emerging as a gigantic spumed wave issuing from the mouth of the Source. Containing all life forms, past present and future, it roared forth as a great wind blowing life force into all existing matter, hurtling into birthed galaxies and worlds lying unfurled and receptive before its enfolding omnipotence.

My own breath meeting that of the Great Uncreate was stilled, remaining silently held in timeless infusion.

9th June 1994

I saw the praise of men ascend delighting the Ear of the Source. It was this sound dearly sought which opened the great Heart of Universal Thought, so that all came to enter into its loving. I saw this Heart beating in perfect synchronicity to the wordless song arising from created beings, amplifying vibrations to resounding expressiveness. Then ravished by love it brought the whole court of heaven into sweet blissfulness

As I looked I saw all creatures stoop low before the threshold of the Uncreate, witnessing the power of that great loving which bid them arise to full glorying. All entered into the Heart which now lay open, receptively inviting man's praisefulness. The revealed chambers of the Heart resembled a great mansion of purest crystal, which caught and held the Cosmic sun in myriad reflected rainbows and within cascading beams of iridescent light. Whenever this energy touched men it shone them to transfigured and and purest spiritual being.

I saw that the hymn of praise sounding always within the deepest part of man's heart, increases in depth and sensitivity as he draws closer to the Heart of the Source. This attracts him powerfully, drawing him always to the sublime point of returning.

Man's heart beat finding resonant and complentary pulsation within the Great heart of the Creator becomes magnetically drawn towards that irresistible gracing which forms an integral part of desirement and resting. Then he beholds within his nature, lying albeit unseen until the moment of grace, the sweet naturing of that Good which originally created him. Then there is realization and knowing that by entering into this divine loving, he will be touched and filled with unending thankfulness and full praising.

I saw the full circling of praise surrounding the throne of the Source. It appeared as a crimson open heart whose throbbing beat enclosed all Creation in sureness of protection and ceaseless loving. I witnessed all men running fast to that Heart which closing around them made them safely into Grace.

GIVE PRAISE, PRAISE, PRAISE TO THE SOURCE.

<u>1Oth June 1994</u>

GIVE
PRAISE
PRAISE PRAISE
PRAISE PRAISE PRAISE
PRAISE PRAISE PRAISE PRAISE
PRAISE PRAISE PRAISE PRAISE PRAISE
PRAISE PRAISE PRAISE PRAISE PRAISE
PRAISE PRAISE PRAISE PRAISE
PRAISE PRAISE PRAISE
PRAISE PRAISE
PRAISE

PRAISE TO THE SOURCE